We dedicate this book to the peer counseling class at Orange Grove Middle School, Hacienda Heights, California, and to their teacher, Mrs. Fran Weimer. Your commitment to peer helping and your assistance in providing us material for this book were both an inspiration and a valued service.

We also dedicate this book to all the peer counselors in other schools who were so gracious to help us in the writing of this book.

ACTING
IT OUT
Junior

Joan Sturkie
Marsh Cassady, PhD

Resource Publications, Inc.
San Jose, California

Editorial director: Kenneth Guentert
Managing editor: Elizabeth J. Asborno
Cover design & production: Huey Lee

Reprint Department
Resource Publications, Inc.
160 E. Virginia Street #290
San Jose, CA 95112-5876

Library of Congress Cataloging in Publication Data
Sturkie, Joan.
      Acting it out junior / Joan Sturkie, Marsh Cassady.
         p.   cm.
      Includes bibliographical references.
      Summary: A collection of short dramatic scenes exploring such issues as AIDS, child abuse, and drugs.
      ISBN 0-89390-240-3
      1. Children—Conduct of life—Drama. 2. Children's plays, American. [1. Conduct of life—Drama. 2. Plays.] I. Cassady, Marsh, 1936-   . II. Title.
      PS3569.T879A28   1992
      812'.54—dc 20   92-29698

96 95 94 93 92 | 5 4 3 2 1

Contents

Introduction

Acting It Out was published two years ago, and we have received a tremendously positive response to it. Undoubtedly, the book meets a need. However, we soon began to get calls from people working with younger kids, asking us to write a sequel addressing specifically the 10-13 age group. This book is a result of their requests.

We wanted these plays to deal with issues which are current and relevant today, so we went to the kids and asked for their help. What a great age group to work with! They talked to us, wrote letters, and sent tapes. They shared their fears, frustrations, joys, and dreams with us in an open, honest way.

Before we began writing the book, we sent an outline and synopsis to the editor for his approval. His comment was, "I can't believe kids this young are having to deal with these types of problems." We assured him that they are. Unfortunately, no part of the country seems to be exempt. All of the plays are based on true stories, but the names, places, and circumstances have been changed in order to respect confidentiality. Some plays may be a combination of different stories.

Because there is no magic wand to wave to make problems go away, we felt the next best thing was to create a situation where kids could talk to each other and share their feelings and needs. Just finding out that other kids have similar problems may in itself be of help. There are a lot of lonely kids out there who think they are the only ones experiencing what they are going through. This book is written to get them talking—first about the situation in the play and their feelings regarding it, and then about how it is relevant to them.

All of the plays do not deal with heavy issues. Some are meant to just get kids thinking about relationships, school, dreams, and goals. In an ever-changing world, some of these young people are asking how they fit in and what contribution they can make to society. The depth of their thinking is apparent when one listens to them.

This book may be used with any 10-to-13-year-old age group, whether it be in a school, church, camp, drug rehabilitation center, private home, eating disorder clinic, halfway house, juvenile detention home, or informal social gathering. It is written so communication can be opened in an easy, nonthreatening way.

Each drama is intentionally short. We wrote it that way so that sufficient time is left for the questions (found at the end) and for the subsequent discussion. The dramas may be used differently at different times. One time you may use a drama to stimulate discussion of a topic or issue. Another time you could use the same drama to provide the beginning of an improvisational scene, in which the actor/participants continue the dialogue without the use of a printed script. Either way (or both) will enhance communication and provide kids with an opportunity to express themselves.

We suggest that the leader explain to the group that when the questions are asked at the end of each play, no one may "put down" someone else, no matter how they answer. When people feel they are not judged or made fun of by what they say, they often take more risk or a greater degree of freedom in expressing their true feelings. Discussing the plays sometimes gives kids a different way to look at an issue and a new appreciation for someone else's point of view. This is particularly helpful in our culturally diverse society.

Thank you for asking for this book. It has been a great pleasure to work with these kids and to share their world with you.

AIDS

Father Has AIDS

*The action occurs in the courtyard of a school
just before morning classes.* **Carol** *is sitting by
herself on a bench. She's crying.*

Natalie: (*Seeing* **Carol** *and walking up to her*) Carol, what's
the matter?

Carol: Nothing.

> **Carol** *looks up and tries to smile as* **Natalie** *sits
> beside her.*

Natalie: Are you OK?

Carol: Oh, Natalie, I don't know what to do. I'm so scared.

Natalie: Do you want to tell me about it?

Carol: It's my father. He has AIDS.

Natalie: Wow! Are you sure?

> **Carol** *nods.*

Natalie: I'm so sorry. (*She puts her arm around Carol's shoulder.*)

Carol: I've known for a long time...that... (*She looks into Natalie's eyes.*) My dad uses drugs. He shoots up, you know? He...he got it from a dirty needle. I'm so afraid... (*She turns away.*)

Natalie: How terrible. I don't know what I'd do if I found out that my father—

Carol: But you don't understand.

Natalie: That your dad...may die?

Carol: It's worse than that, Natalie. Don't you see?

Natalie: What do you mean?

Carol: Mom could die too.

Natalie: Oh, Carol.

Carol: I mean how is AIDS caught...transmitted? (*She closes her eyes for a moment and then opens them again.*) People sharing needles and...having sex without—

Natalie: Unprotected? Without a condom.

Carol: Yes. What am I going to do? I don't know what to do.

Natalie: Have you talked to your mom about this? Has she been tested? Maybe she's OK.

Carol: Do you think so?

Natalie: I don't know. But Mr. Collins in health class said that just because one partner has AIDS, it doesn't mean the other one has it too. Don't you remember?

Carol: I guess so.

Natalie: Babies can even be born to HIV positive mothers and be OK.

Carol: No matter what, my dad's still going to die. Unless someone finds a cure. And they're not going to find a cure that soon.

> **Rob** *sees the two girls and walks over.*

Rob: Hey, you two, what's wrong?

> **Natalie** *looks at* **Carol.**

Rob: (*Turning to* **Carol**) Are you OK?

Carol: No, I'm not OK.

Rob: Can you tell me what's wrong?

> **Carol** *shakes her head.*

Natalie: Rob, do you think maybe you should—

Rob: Should what?

Natalie: Maybe Natalie doesn't feel like talking.

Carol: It's OK. We've been friends since first grade. (*She turns to* **Rob**.) It's my father, Rob. I just found out he has AIDS.

Rob: Geez, Carol, you're sure?

Carol: Yes! You know how he is; we've talked about it. He uses drugs. He's been using them for years. Mom did too, I guess. But she stopped. She tried to get him to stop too, but he wouldn't.

Rob: How long has he had—

Carol: I don't know. He's been feeling bad and finally went to be tested. What he really has is ARC—AIDS Related Complex. But the doctor says it's pretty close to being full-blown AIDS.

Natalie: But your mom hasn't been tested?

Carol: She went yesterday, to county health. They have free tests. (*She breaks into sobs.*)

Rob: Did she find out anything?

Carol: No. Mom has to go back next Wednesday. If they both die, I don't know what I'll do. I don't know what's going to happen to me. (*She shakes her head.*) I'm being selfish. I should be thinking about Dad and Mom, not about me.

Rob: What about your grandparents? Don't you have grandparents?

Carol: Only my grandma. She has arthritis and can't get around very well. So how could she take care of us? My brothers and me? (*She looks from* **Rob** *to* **Natalie**) What am I going to do? What's going to happen to me?

Questions for Discussion

1. Do you think Natalie helped Carol? How? What else could she have done?

2. Carol mentions two ways of contracting AIDS. What are they? What other ways may a person contract AIDS?

3. Carol recognizes that her father will die if a cure is not found for AIDS. How can she show support and understanding to him?

4. Do you think Rob asks too many questions? Is there another way he can let her know that he cares? If so, how?

5. Is Carol being unrealistic in thinking both of her parents might die? Is her concern for herself unwarranted?

Can It Happen to Us?

The action occurs at the community recreation center. **Theresa** *has just left with a much older boy, a high school dropout named* **Wardell**, *who is known to live in the fast lane—using drugs, drinking, having sex with a lot of different partners. A group of her classmates, including* **Bobbi, Kathy, Matt,** *and* **Jim** *have just finished playing in a co-ed softball game.*

Jim: I don't know why Theresa'd be so dumb as to go off with someone like that. I always thought she was smart.

Kathy: I don't think being smart has anything to do with it.

Matt: What do you mean?

Kathy: Well, you know. Dating an older guy. Having him pay attention to a girl who's only in middle school. Who wouldn't be flattered?

Bobbi: Well, I for one wouldn't.

Kathy: Oh, come on, Bobbi, you can't tell me you wouldn't be thrilled to have an older guy ask you for a date.

Bobbi: My mom would kill me.

Jim: I've heard all kinds of things about that guy Wardell, you know?

Matt: What do you mean?

Jim: Where have you been, man? He has the worst reputation of anyone in the neighborhood.

Matt: I guess.

Kathy: He smokes grass. I know that for sure. And a girl who lives on my block said he asked her to do coke one night.

Bobbi: You mean she did?

Kathy: No, she didn't. But what about Theresa? Is she going to be able to say no?

Bobbi: I'm sure he shoots up too. He may even offer her the needle.

Jim: But it isn't just that he does drugs. He's into all kinds of things. He's been in Juvenile Hall at least two times that I know of. And Theresa's pretty innocent.

Matt: Well, everyone knows that Wardell...well, I know a girl he's gotten pregnant.

Bobbi: What if Theresa got pregnant? Her parents would kill her. They'd kill her if they even found out she went with this creep.

Kathy: Creep! He's not a creep, that's the problem. He's handsome, and he always has a lot of money.

Bobbi: Yeah, from selling drugs.

Kathy: I know, and that's certainly not too bright, is it? Theresa just didn't think this thing through. She figured it was glamorous. Maybe she even wanted to make us jealous.

Bobbi: Not me. I don't know what I'd do if I got pregnant.

Jim: That isn't the worst of it. The thing I'd worry about would be AIDS.

Bobbi: I didn't think of that.

Jim: From what everyone knows about Wardell, he's certainly the type who could get it.

Matt: And so could every girl he's had sex with.

Jim: Man, it's really scary. I was talking to my folks about it. About AIDS, and you know we're kind of the AIDS generation.

Matt: (*Laughing*) What's that supposed to mean?

Jim: It's true, Matt. We're the ones born into it. I mean it wasn't around when our parents were young.

Bobbi: You're right, Jim. You really have to be careful, don't you?

Kathy: If you're going to use crack or heroin or stuff like that. Or if you're...well, sexually active.

Matt: It's scary. I mean anyone can have it. My dad said it used to be only homosexual men.

Bobbi: Yeah, I've heard that. But I wonder if it's true.

Kathy: What do you mean?

Bobbi: If it started out with homosexuals, how come other people are getting it now?

Jim: My social studies teacher said in Africa it's more heterosexuals. Not gay guys at all.

Kathy: It means anyone could get it, I guess.

Matt: If you're reckless.

Bobbi: Like Theresa maybe.

Jim: Yeah, like Theresa. Anytime there's a little pressure. I mean, how strong is any of us? Are we sure we can stand up to the pressure?

Kathy: I don't plan to take drugs or go with just any guy who happens to ask me.

Matt: Yeah, but what if you're with a group of kids who're all doing drugs? And you're the only one who's not.

Jim: I like to think I'm strong enough to say no. But am I? I'm not so sure.

Questions for Discussion

1. Why do you think Theresa wants to go out with an older boy who has a bad reputation?

2. Theresa's friends seem to know all about the things Wardell did. Do you think Theresa knows also?

3. Do you think she thinks she can say no to drugs and/or sex? Do you think she can?

4. Do you think students in your class will become HIV positive before they get out of high school?

5. What can be done to keep your peers and yourself from getting AIDS?

CHILD ABUSE

Too Old to be Abused

The action occurs on the steps of the school.
Mary *is waiting for* **Trudy,**
since the two of them always ride
home together with Mary's mom.

Mary: (*Seeing* **Trudy** *coming out the door*) Hi, Trudy. Ready to go?

Trudy: Yeah, my English teacher wanted to talk to me about something on my last paper. Sorry I'm late.

Mary: That's OK. I— (*She notices bruises on Trudy's arm.*) What happened to you? Did you fall down or something?

Trudy: It's nothing. It happens all the time.

Mary: What do you mean? What happens all the time?

Trudy: I told you it's nothing. It doesn't matter. Let's just forget it, OK?

Mary: Did somebody do this to you?

Trudy: (*Laughing*) Yeah, and you should have seen the other person.

Mary: Did you get into a fight with someone? On the way to school or something?

Trudy: Why does it matter, Trudy? I told you it was nothing. Why can't you just leave it alone?

Mary: (*Shrugs*) I'm just worried about you, that's all. We're friends, and friends are supposed to care.

Trudy: All right. Mom and I got into a fight. Like I said, it happens all the time.

Mary: That's child abuse. I'm going to have to report it. (**Trudy** gives her a look of disgust.) I mean it. I learned in my peer helping class that I have to report things like this. The law states that child abuse must be reported.

Trudy: For heaven's sake, Mary. I'm sorry you even noticed. Just leave me alone, will you? It's nothing, OK?

Mary: Well, it's child abuse and—

Trudy: It's not child abuse, you know!

Mary: What do you mean?

Trudy: I'm in middle school, Mary. I'm not a child, and neither are you. Or maybe you think you're still a baby.

Mary: Come on, Trudy, I'm just trying to help you.

Trudy: No, what you're doing is trying to make trouble. I'm old enough to fight my own battles. I don't need someone doing it for me. (*She sighs.*) You're my friend, Mary. You should understand about things like this.

Mary: What do you mean?

Trudy: Don't you ever fight with your parents?

Mary: Argue, sure, everyone does. But they don't hit me. Dad spanked me once a long time ago. And he said he was sorry. But maybe I deserved it. I was playing with his computer when I wasn't supposed to and wiped out an important file. One he'd spent hours on for his work.

Trudy: Well, maybe my family's different. Maybe we settle things a different way, if you know what I mean.

Mary: I'm not kidding, Trudy. I have to report it. Anytime an adult does things like that, it's child abuse.

Trudy: You must think my mother's a terrible person, right?

Mary: I didn't say that.

Trudy: But you meant it.

Mary: I'm sorry.

Trudy: Then it's settled.

Mary: No.

Trudy: Hey, girl, what is your problem? I said I'm not a child. I can take care of myself.

Mary: My peer helping teacher says that under the law a person's considered a child till they reach the age of eighteen. He really stressed how important this is. So no matter what you say or how grownup you think you are—

Trudy: (*Trying to laugh it off*) If you think this is bad, you should have seen my mom.

Mary: What do you mean?

Trudy: OK, if you want to know so much, she has a lot more bruises than I do.

Mary: What?

Trudy: That's right, Mary. So are you going to report my whole family?

Mary: I don't understand.

Trudy: I just told you. I have bruises; my mom has bruises.

Mary: Do you mean you and your mom got into fights and you hurt each other?

Trudy: I can't believe this. I mean you act like you're totally innocent. You're the one who needs to grow up. (*She starts down the steps and turns.*) I'll walk home. I don't need any more of this.

Mary: Trudy, please. Don't do that. It's a long ways.

Trudy: (*Turning back*) Will you promise not to report this? I'm really not a child, you know. Look, you want to know something funny? I weigh almost as much as my mother. So maybe you should report me instead of her. Don't you see? I can take care of myself. I don't need anyone trying to fight my battles.

Mary: I know it's hard to accept, Trudy. But I don't have any choice.

Trudy: Yeah, right.

Mary: Well, I don't.

Trudy: Then why don't you drop that class?

Mary: It's not just the class. Anyone witnessing child abuse or seeing the results should report it.

Trudy: Hey, Mary, give it up. I always figured you were my friend. I never took you for such a...a... (*She turns away.*) Oh, forget it.

Questions for Discussion

1. Is Mary being nosy? Do you think she should have kept questioning Trudy like she did?

2. Do you agree with Mary that Trudy is involved in child abuse? Mary states that a person is considered a child until age eighteen. Is that the same age your state has for its child abuse reporting?

3. Why do you think Trudy is so opposed to having Mary report what she has seen? Is she concerned for her mother or herself?

4. As a peer helper, Mary seems to take her responsibilities seriously. What other things have you noticed about peer helpers?

5. Trudy says she thought Mary was her friend. Would a friend report another friend?

Father's Little Princess

The action occurs in a peer helping class.

Jeanne: Is something bothering you, Sue?

Sue: Yes. But I don't know if I want to talk about it.

Billy: I think I can understand how you feel. Remember that time I didn't show up for practice cause my dog was sick and because of it I got kicked off the team? Well, it helped me to talk about it. It helped me see every side—

Sue: I wish it was something like that. But it isn't. It's a lot worse. It's...well, I'm kind of ashamed. I don't want anyone to be hurt.

Diane: Is it you who's going to be hurt?

Kevin: What Diane means, I think, is that if it's something that will hurt you to talk about—

Sue: You don't understand. No one understands. (*She looks around the classroom.*) You're all so lucky. Nothing like this would ever happen to you. I wish it wouldn't happen to me.

Jeanne: You feel like you're alone in whatever it is. Is that right?

Sue: It's my father. I don't know if I can say it.

Billy: We're here to listen—and to be nonjudgmental.

Sue: OK. He calls me his Little Princess.

Jeanne: Is that so bad?

Sue: No, it's not so bad. It's just...wow, this is hard. I want to tell you, but I don't. Do you see what I mean?

Billy: Yes, I do. Acknowledging what I did last week was difficult.

Sue: But like I said, I can't imagine this happening to anyone else but me. I feel really alone in this. No one else has a father like... (*She starts to cry.*)

Diane: It really hurts to talk about it.

Sue: Yes! I hate to be alone with him. And I try not to be because of what happens. (*She rubs a hand across her eyes.*) And I feel it's all my fault. I mean I must be a terrible person. Or else why would he do those things?

Diane: (*Softly*) What sort of things does he do, Sue?

Sue: He... He likes to get me alone.

Jeanne: I think I understand.

Sue: Do you?

Jeanne: I think so.

Sue: It started out a long time ago. Whenever Mom went shopping or to a meeting or somewhere. Sometimes when she had to work late, and Daddy and I were alone.

Kevin: It's OK, Sue. We care about you; you know that.

Sue: Thanks, Kevin. I know. (*She looks down at her hands, not making eye contact with anyone.*) At first, he'd just hold me. That's all, just hold me. And hug me. And then he started kissing me.

Diane: Kissing you?

Sue: Not the kind of kiss a father's supposed to... This is so hard. 'Cause like I said, I think it's all my fault. Like I'm a terrible person. And if I tell you all this, you're going to have to report it. I know you have to. And then what's my mom going to think?

Billy: She doesn't know?

Sue: How could she know? She's never there when...when he starts these things.

Jeanne: You said he just kisses you?

Sue: Well, at first. Then he started rubbing my arms and my back and pretty soon where...where he shouldn't. And he wanted me to...do things to him.

Diane: You remember when we studied about child abuse—sexual child abuse?

Sue: I know. It has to be reported. And then everything's going to change. But it's getting so bad. I mean the last time we were...we were alone, he wanted to go up to his room and he asked me to...

Kevin: This must be awfully hard.

Sue: You don't know how hard it is. Even harder than I imagined. But I'm glad I'm telling you about it. I'm glad it's out in the open. (*She starts to cry.*) I couldn't live with it anymore. I couldn't.

Diane: It's OK, Sue. It must have been a terrible thing to keep to yourself.

Sue: But I love my dad. And what does that make me? Maybe he was right to treat me like that. I still love him. I can't help it, but I love him.

Questions for Discussion

1. Sue feels all alone and thinks what has happened to her has never happened to anyone else in the class. Do you think she is right?

2. If incest happens to one out of five people, how many people in your class would statistically be involved?

3. Do you think Sue is correct when she says her mother does not know?

4. Why is reporting sexual child abuse so important? Name other people in the family who may benefit from the reporting.

5. What do you think will happen to Sue's father?

6. Sue states that she loves her father. Do most children love their parents if they are being abused?

I Just Want to Help You Grow Up

The action occurs in the social hall of a church.

Rev. Carson: How old are you now, Barry? Just about ready to go into high school, aren't you?

Barry: That's right.

Rev. Carson: Almost all grown up.

Barry: (*Laughing*) I wish that's what my parents thought.

Rev. Carson: What do you mean?

Barry: They treat me like a little kid.

Rev. Carson: I wouldn't treat you like a kid, Barry. I think you're almost a man. A handsome man too.

Barry: Sure. (*Smiling*) A young whippersnapper. That's what my great-grandpa says.

25

Rev. Carson: That's what my folks called me too. I'd forgotten all about it. (*He looks at* **Barry**.) But like I said, you're almost a man. I'll bet you've noticed a lot of changes, haven't you?

Barry: I don't know what you mean, Rev. Carson.

Rev. Carson: In your body. All those raging hormones. They do all kinds of wonderful things. You can tell me about it.

Barry: You mean like my voice starting to change?

Rev. Carson: Well, that's just a part of it. There are other things that are much more important.

Barry: (*Beginning to feel uncomfortable*) I don't understand.

Rev. Carson: I'd be glad to show you.

Barry: What!

Rev. Carson: Now don't be afraid. I don't mean any harm.

Barry: I think I'd better go now. My mom will be here to pick me up.

Rev. Carson: (*Looking at his watch*) Not for a while yet. Anyway, I'm glad to have this chance to talk with you. And I'd like you to think about what I said.

Barry: About...about changes in my body.

Rev. Carson: Yes, and I'd like to help you understand. I'd like you to stop in and talk about it more later. My housekeeper will be gone all day tomorrow. What do you think?

Barry: I don't know.

Rev. Carson: I'd certainly like to explore this further. You think about it, Barry, and we'll talk again.

Scene ii

The action occurs in Barry's room.
George *is his best friend.*

George: You've got to be kidding. Rev. Carson. You're making it up.

Barry: I'm not. That's what he said, and I'm scared. I mean, Mom and Dad warned me about things like that.

George: Maybe he did just want to talk.

Barry: Come on, George. Whose side are you on? I always thought you were my friend.

George: So what are you going to do?

Barry: Nothing.

George: But if you're scared, you have to do something about it.

Barry: The guy didn't do anything to me, man. What am I supposed to do?

George: Could you talk to your parents?

Barry: And tell them what? That Rev. Carson asked me about changes in my body. They'd think he was just concerned, that he wanted to help me understand what it's like to become a man.

George: Maybe that's all he did want.

Barry: So has he talked to you?

George: No.

Barry: Well, you're five months older than I am, right?

George: Yeah, so what?

Barry: So why didn't he try to talk to you?

George: I don't know. Maybe he will.

Barry: I don't think so. My older brother never said anything about something like this. And we've been going to that church all my life. And Rev. Carson's been there for a long time.

George: Yeah. So what's your next move?

Barry: I can't stop going to church. You know how my parents are. And I can't stay away from Rev. Carson forever, can I?

George: Wow, I'm glad it isn't happening to me. I don't know what I'd do.

Barry: Yeah, well, how about that movie? We better get going if we want to get there on time.

Questions for Discussion

1. Is Barry right in being concerned? Can any person, even a minister, be a child abuser?

2. Do you think Barry should tell his parents? Do you think George should tell his parents what Barry has told him?

3. Barry mentions an older brother. Do you think this brother may have a secret he has never told anyone?

4. George says, "But if you're scared, you have to do something about it." What should Barry do?

5. Do you think adults generally would believe kids over a minister, or visa versa?

COMMUNICATION

Parents Do Not Communicate Love

Allison *and* **Jake** *are sitting at a picnic table on campus before the start of morning classes.*

Allison: I wish my mom and dad would just tell me once that they love me. I mean, they never have.

Jake: Well, my dad doesn't say it much anymore, I guess, because I'm growing up. But he used to. (*He smiles.*) I can still remember when I was a little kid. Dad'd come home from work, pick me up and swing me around. And he always told me he loved me. Mom still does.

Allison: It's not like they don't do things for me. They do, but they never tell me how they feel.

Jake: Maybe that's their way of saying it.

Allison: Yes, but it's not the same thing. I mean, they got me a new stereo for my birthday, and my other one was only a couple of years old. And it was perfectly OK.

Jake: I wish I had a stereo of my own—I mean like the one you have. I have a little table model, but it's not the same.

Allison: You don't understand, Jake. I'd be glad to trade all the stuff they give me just once to hear them say they love me.

Jake: Some people just aren't like that.

Allison: Well, they should be.

Jake: You really feel bad about this, don't you?

Allison: Wouldn't you?

Jake: I suppose I would, but I can't imagine not being told I'm loved.

Allison: Well, I often think it's a kind of bribe, you know? They don't love me, and they feel guilty about it. So they buy me everything anyone ever could want. And I'm supposed to accept it and not tell anyone how things really are.

Jake: Do you honestly think that's the way they feel?

Allison: No, I suppose not. Well, actually, I don't know. You've met my mother.

Jake: I've met her.

Allison: So do you envy me for the way things are?

Jake: I guess not.

Allison: If only they'd listen to me. Yeah, they give me all kinds of lessons—piano, ballet, painting. They send me to the best camps—but I think it's just to get me out of their way. It's like I'm intruding on their lives...like they don't want me around.

Jake: Come on, Allison. I'm sure they wouldn't do all those things for you if they didn't love you.

Allison: They never talk to me. They never listen to what I have to say. I mean, if I want to say something or ask them something, they have better things to do. "Hush, dear, I want to watch this show," my mom says, and it's some dumb thing about Africa or the Civil War or something. Or she says I'm interrupting what she and dad are talking about.

Jake: Is your dad like that too?

Allison: He never wants to listen either. And he never talks to me except to tell me to help mom clean up the house or do my chores.

Jake: But they're always at concerts to hear you play in the band. They're at all the school functions.

Allison: Maybe because it looks good.

Jake: This really bothers you, doesn't it?

Allison: Everyone thinks we're one great family. That my folks are examples of what all parents should be. But they're not. I shouldn't let it bother me, I suppose. But it does.

Jake: What can you do about it?

Allison: In what way?

Jake: Can you talk to them about it?

Allison: Jake!

Jake: Dumb, question huh? That's what you've been saying, that you can't talk. Is there anything else you can do? Like talk to a relative—an aunt or uncle or your grandparents? To tell them how things are? To ask them to talk to your folks.

Allison: You've got to be kidding. Mom and Dad would only get mad.

Jake: Well, maybe you just have to accept it. I don't know. You won't be with them forever.

Allison: But it seems like forever.

Jake: I don't know what else to say.

Allison: I know, Jake. And thanks. At least I have a friend who'll listen, even if my mom and dad won't.

Questions for Discussion

1. Why do you think Allison's parents do not tell her they love her? Or do you think they do, nonverbally?

2. What can Allison do to get her parents to listen?

3. What have you done to open up communication with your parents? Talk about the things you found to be most effective.

4. Why is hearing the words, "I love you," so important?

5. Jake says, "I don't know what else to say." What else could he have said or done?

Fighting: A Form of Communication?

The action takes place in a peer helping class.

Ben: No matter what I try to say, my brother won't listen. He always just wants to pick a fight.

Josie: No matter what you try?

Ben: Yeah, right. It's like Tommy hates me. I mean I know kids always fight with their brothers and sisters, but it seems like they can get along some of the time.

Brad: My brother and I certainly get into it a lot of times. And so do my sisters. It just about drives Mom and Dad nuts.

Ben: But you do get along some of the time, don't you?

Brad: I guess so. Sure, we do.

Ben: Well, it's like if I say anything, Tommy gets mad. Anything at all. Like "Hi, Tom, how you doing?" or

"Ready for school?" Things that shouldn't be a problem, right?

Terri: Are you saying Tommy becomes angry even at things like that?

Ben: Yeah, no matter what I say.

Brad: What if he says something to you first?

Ben: What do you mean?

Brad: Doesn't he ever talk to you first?

Ben: I don't know; I guess so.

Brad: Can you think of a time?

Ben: No, well, yeah.

Josie: Do you want to tell us about it?

Ben: Well, last night, for instance. He asked me to help him with his math. He's in fifth grade.

Josie: Did you?

Ben: It was a bad time. I was trying to do my own homework.

Terri: So what did you do? What happened?

Ben: We got into it again. (*Shrugs*) OK, this time maybe it was my fault. I told him to butt out, and so he started yelling.

Terri: What did you do then?

Ben: I got mad.

Josie: Can you think of any time you two have tried to talk when you didn't get into a fight?

Ben: It's hard to think... OK. A few days ago. It was Tommy's birthday, and I got him this record I knew he'd really been wanting.

Brad: So you don't hate him or anything.

Ben: (*Looking shocked*) Of course, I don't hate him. He's my brother.

Brad: You know what? I have two sisters, both older than me. And they hate each other's guts. They really do. Mom and Dad really get upset about it all the time.

Ben: Tommy's not that bad, as kid brothers go. Other than the fighting, he's OK.

Josie: You're really concerned about this, aren't you?

Ben: Wouldn't you be?

Josie: I don't have any brothers or sisters. I'm an only child.

Ben: I know I've learned a lot of things about getting along. In this class, I mean. About respecting opinions and not judging. Stuff like that.

Brad: What are you saying, Ben?

Ben: Shouldn't I be able to get along then? I mean, the only kind of communication Tom and I have is fighting. Except on special occasions. It's making my parents crazy. They're at their wits' end.

Terri: Have you talked to them about it?

Ben: I don't think they'd listen.

Terri: Oh?

Ben: Like I said, they hate what's going on. They don't want to hear about it.

Terri: Are you sure?

Ben: You mean really talk to them about it? I don't know. Maybe if Tommy and I both said something.

Terri: How does your brother feel about all this?

Ben: I have no idea. It can't be fun. It's way past that. I mean, often there are a lot of things I'd like to talk to him about. You know, about teachers and classes. Give him pointers.

Josie: It seems to me from what I hear that you care a lot about your brother.

Ben: Of course I do. He's family. He's all I've got except Mom and Dad. And I don't even know how all this started.

Brad: Is that important?

Ben: How it started?

Brad: Yeah.

Ben: Maybe not; I don't know. It somehow got started and then became worse. It's just something that happened. I guess what's important is doing something to stop it.

Terri: Do you have any other options you haven't tried?

Ben: One thing I thought of.

Brad: What is it?

Ben: If one of you guys might talk to him. I mean I know some of you know him. Tell him how I feel. Tell him I'm not mad at him. I don't hate him. Tell him maybe that fighting is a sort of communication. But not the best kind. Maybe even the worst kind.

Terri: Do you think that's a good idea?

Ben: OK, not really. I have to try to get through to him by myself. And I don't know how. I wish I did.

Questions for Discussion

1. Do you think the fighting between Ben and his brother is normal in a family? What makes it normal or abnormal?

2. Why did Ben not want to help Tommy with his math? Should he have stopped what he was doing and helped him?

3. Ben says that he doesn't think his parents will listen. How could he elicit help from them?

4. Ben reveals his problem to a peer helping class. How could they help him?

5. Do you think fighting is a form of communication?

CROSS-CULTURAL
DIVERSITY

More Alike Than Different

The action takes place in a peer helping class.

Jason: I'm glad that you shared your feelings this morning, Leng. I never imagined that you could ever dread taking a test. Making good grades seems to be a part of who you are.

Leng: That's the problem. It's not a part of who I am. I study a lot and do OK on my tests, but I get knots in my stomach before each one. Sometimes I even break out in a cold sweat.

Jason: I would never have suspected. I guess you seem much more human to me now that I know you have some of the same feelings as the rest of us.

Leng: You mean I'm not the Asian kid who has it all together like the typical stereotype.

Jason: Something like that. You just always seemed so cool in science class that I thought we operated on different planets.

Leng: (*Laughs*) I know what you mean about operating on different planets. I had the same feeling about you until I listened to what you had to say in this class.

Jason: Really?

Leng: Sure. You joke around in science class so much I thought you never could have a serious thought. I really couldn't relate to you because in my eyes you were immune to the fears and frustrations I felt. Now I know that we both have them. You just cover yours better by joking around.

Maria: I appreciate what the two of you are sharing. I guess when I entered this class, I saw both of you as being somewhat alike and me as being very different.

Jason: (*Puzzled*) Leng and me as being alike?

Maria: Sure. You both dressed nice. You both seemed very confident, maybe in different ways—you were confident in a quiet, strong way, Leng, and (*looking at Jason*) you were never at a loss for words.

Leng: Why did you see yourself different from the two of us? I've always admired you in this class. I know I could never carry the load you do.

Maria: But what I do is expected of me culturally.

Jason: I know people from Mexico who don't spend nearly as much time with their family as you have to.

Maria: Maybe that's because there aren't younger kids in the family or grandparents who live next door.

Leng: I understand that the family is important in your culture, but having to go straight home from school every day to help out with little kids and grandparents would get me down.

Maria: It gets me down sometimes too, but they are my family and I love them.

Leng: I can't imagine when you ever have time to get your homework done. You must be exhausted by the time you help with dinner for your grandparents and then bathe and get all your younger brothers and sisters to bed.

Maria: No one in my family has ever been to college, so education isn't one of their top priorities. I get enough of my homework done to pass all my classes, but sometimes I do wish I had more time to do it. I really like school.

Leng: You're so naturally smart that if you had more time to apply yourself, you'd probably make the best grades in the class.

Maria: Oh, I don't think so. But it makes me feel good to know that you think that.

Stephanie: Listening to the three of you talk makes me realize how glad I am to be in this class. All of you come from different cultures that may have different expectations, but basically you're all the same—deep down, I mean.

Reed: I agree with you, Stephanie. I know I won't be so quick to judge other people from other cultures now.

Stephanie: You mean you won't stereotype them?

Reed: I'll know better.

Questions for Discussion

1. Why do you think there is a tendency to stereotype people?

2. What ways can you think of for kids from different cultures to get to know and come to a better understanding of each other?

3. Why do you think Jason is surprised to learn that Leng feels anxious before taking a test?

4. What are some things that Leng, Jason, and Maria all have in common?

5. What lesson has Reed learned from listening to others in the class?

DATING

Mother Says I'm Too Young

The action takes place in the school cafeteria at lunchtime. **Dawn, Tina, Sally, Tim, James** *and* **Geoff** *are sharing a table.*

Dawn: Are you all going to the Christmas dance?

Sally: James and I are going.

James: That's right. My mom's going to drive us. How about you, Tim?

Tim: I guess so. I asked Marie, and her mom said it's OK.

James: How are you getting there?

Tim: I'm not sure yet. We have to work something out.

James: We have a van with plenty of room. I'm sure it would be OK if you go with us.

Dawn: What about you, Tina?

Tina: (*Upset*) My mom says I can't go.

Sally: I thought you and Geoff were going together.

Geoff: I thought so too. What's this all about?

Tina: I'm sorry, Geoff. I meant to tell you, but it didn't seem the right time.

Sally: How come you can't go?

Tina: Mom says I'm too young. I'm not allowed to start dating till I'm a junior in high school.

James: A junior. That's a long time. You'll be what...sixteen?

Tina: That's right.

Geoff: I thought it was all planned. I mean I asked, and you said it was OK.

Tina: I thought so too.

Dawn: Gee, my mom was married by the time she was sixteen. (*Smiles.*) Of course, she says I'd better not even think of anything like that.

Tim: What's your mom got against dating?

Tina: It's not that. It's just that...

James: Just what?

Tina: She says kids our age would be playing with fire. We don't have any control or something like that.

Geoff: Gosh, Tina, it's just a date. We're not getting married.

James: (*Laughs*) Well, you could never prove it by my mom. She feels exactly the same way. But when I said she could take us and pick us up right afterward, there was no problem.

Tina: I don't like not being trusted. I just really don't.

Dawn: Are you sure that's it, that she doesn't trust you?

Tina: What do you mean?

Dawn: Well, my mom says she just hates to see me grow up.

Tim: My mom too, I guess. But it's going to happen whether anyone likes it or not.

Tina: I'm really angry about all this. I told her everyone else was going, and she said she'd heard that argument before. But everyone is going, all my friends.

Sally: I'd be mad too. I've been looking forward to this for weeks. And if my mom told me I couldn't go, I don't know what I'd do.

Tina: I wish I could sneak out. I'd do it. (*She turns to* **Geoff.**) I'm sorry. Mom only told me last night. She said she and Dad talked about it. I know I should have called you.

Geoff: She doesn't want me seeing you at all?

Tina: It's like she's living in the Middle Ages.

Sally: When do you think kids should be allowed to date? Really date, I mean. Go out together—like to movies or something. Not just to school games or school dances.

Tim: (*Laughing*) Well, personally, I'm not ready for all that yet. My wallet couldn't stand the shock.

Geoff: You have a point, I guess. High school kids have an easier time getting jobs. They can pay for it.

Tina: It doesn't have to be anything expensive.

Dawn: Well, I certainly got a lecture from my mom about it. She thinks she knows all about it. See, I was born when she was just seventeen, so she says we're close to the same age. But it's different now, no matter what she says. Everything is different. It's a whole new generation, and parents just don't know how things are.

Tina: Maybe, but they certainly think they do. Maybe Mom thinks she can't trust me 'cause she couldn't trust herself.

Dawn: Tina! You shouldn't say things like that about your mother.

Tina: I guess not. Well, OK, I know I shouldn't. But how would you feel if you were the one who couldn't go?

Dawn: Not so good, I guess. But I'm not sure how far my own mom trusts me.

Sally: I don't think it's so much that Mom doesn't trust me. She had a hard time accepting that I want to go, that I'm old enough. Even though I convinced her to let me do it. She still thinks of me as a little girl.

Tim: What do you mean?

Sally: She doesn't think I'm ready yet. She doesn't think kids our age are old enough to date. She thinks it's all tied in with peer pressure.

Tim: Sometimes I think maybe it is.

Sally: What are you saying, Tim? That you really don't want to go?

Tim: Not me, but other kids.

Sally: Like who?

Geoff: Me for one. (*He glances at* **Tina.**) Now that it's off, Tina, I can say it. I'm kind of relieved. I mean—

Dawn: Just what do you mean!

Geoff: Don't get me wrong, Tina. We've been friends for a long time.

Tina: And you want a friend instead of a date?

Geoff: Well, maybe I do. I don't know. Maybe the dance would be fun. You know my brother's only a couple of years younger than me. And you know what, he's still playing with toy cars. What's funny, I remember when I did that too. It wasn't that long ago. And then one day I put the cars away and didn't take them out anymore. I'd outgrown them. But am I ready for dating? I'm not sure.

Dawn: Well, I am. It's going to be fun.

Tina: I know, and I'm going to miss out on all of it.

Dawn: Isn't there a way to get your mother to change her mind?

Tina: I don't think so. I've pretty much given up on it.

The bell rings, and the students start to collect
their trays and dishes.

Questions for Discussion

1. Tina says she will not be allowed to date until she is sixteen. How old do you think a person should be before he or she is at the right age to start dating? Do you think your parents agree with you?

2. Tina states that she doesn't like not being trusted. Do you think her mother does not trust her? Or are there other reasons for not wanting her to start dating? What could be some of those reasons?

3. Dawn says, "It's a whole new generation, and parents just don't know how things are." Do you agree or disagree? Why?

4. Discuss Geoff's mixed feelings about dating. Can you identify with these feelings?

5. Talk about social activities you and your peers (both male and female) can do together if your parents do not allow you to date at this age.

Peer Pressure to Date

The action occurs in Mr. Hoskins' social studies class, where the students have been talking about dating and marriage customs. The discussion now turns to the current situation.

Mr. Hoskins: So you see there are a lot of strange customs associated with dating and marriage.

John: Maybe our own customs are kind of weird too.

The other members of the class laugh.

Mr. Hoskins: (*Smiling*) You may have a point. Would you care to explain what you mean, John?

John: Sure, maybe in some other places in the world, people start dating and even...getting together at twelve or thirteen. Now that's weird to us, but what would they think of our customs here where the guy has to dish out all the money for everything?

Suzie: You're back in the dark ages, John. Haven't you heard of Women's Lib?

Justin: Haven't you girls heard of Women's Lib?

Suzie: What do you mean by that?

Mike: I think he means that the guy still has to pay for the date.

Mr. Hoskins: You have brought up an interesting topic. Our own customs here in North America.

Valerie: What's so interesting about it?

Mr. Hoskins: To the rest of the world, some of the things we do must look pretty strange.

Mike: In what way?

Mr. Hoskins: Why don't you answer that yourself, Mike?

Mike: Well, I suppose we start dating a lot younger than they do some places. (*He glances at* **John.**) At least some of us do.

John: What's that supposed to mean?

Mike: Come on, John, you've never been on a date in your life.

John: So what?

Mike: So what are you waiting for? Your mama to give you permission?

John: Now just wait a minute.

Mr. Hoskins: All right, class. That's enough.

John: Mr. Hoskins, I'd like to answer, OK?

Mr. Hoskins: Go ahead.

John: (*He looks from one face to another.*) You're right. I don't go on dates. And I don't plan to go on dates. So why does that make you all better than me?

Suzie: Look, John, I don't go on dates either. Mom won't let me. She says I'm not old enough.

Mike: But your mom would let you, wouldn't she, John?

John: I guess so. I'm just not interested.

Mike: You're not trying to tell us something? I mean, you're not one of those guys who...likes other guys, are you?

John: I'm not gay, if that's what you mean. And anyhow, guys like that date other guys, right?

Everyone laughs.

Mr. Hoskins: Get to your point, John.

John: I don't have time to date.

Mr. Hoskins: Do you want to explain that?

John: Yeah, Mom and Dad have their hearts set on my being a doctor. (*He shrugs.*) And maybe that's what I want too.

Justin: Doctors date. People who are going to be doctors date. The son of the people who live next door is in medical school. And he's engaged. He must think it's all right.

John: OK, you all know I'm not the brightest guy in the world. Even the brightest guy in the room, for that matter.

Mike: Your grades look pretty good to me.

John: Well, that's because I study.

Justin: I never could figure that. I mean you're not a nerd. Not like some guys I know. (*He looks at* **Mike.**)

Mike: Yeah? Well who's the one with the thick glasses?

Mr. Hoskins: All right, you two, knock it off. (*He looks toward* **John.**) What were you saying?

John: I don't have time. I have to study. Hard. I'm not like a genius or anything.

Justin: Don't we just know it.

John: (*Giving him a mock frown.*) Anyhow, I have a lot of pressure on me if I want to get into the best colleges and go on to med school.

Mike: College! That's years off. Who even thinks about college?

Suzie: My parents already want me to go to an Ivy League School. They started talking about it when I was born.

Valerie: You're kidding.

Suzie: I'm not. (*Shrugs*) But like Mike says, it's a long way off. It doesn't even seem real. I know I'll probably go. My folks have been saving already to send me, but—

John: Anyhow, I'm just explaining. Maybe I'd like to date. I haven't thought about it much, but I can't afford to let my grades slide.

Valerie: Mom told me that colleges don't even look at grades except for the last couple of years of high school.

Mr. Hoskins: Well, certainly more than that.

John: Do you think I'm dumb for studying like I do, Mr. Hoskins? Is that what you're saying?

Mr. Hoskins: I'm sorry if I gave that impression, John. It isn't what I meant, not at all. I think it's great that you're developing good study habits as young as you are.

Suzie: Well, I don't. What kind of a life is that, without doing other things? Without having fun. There's a lot of life beyond schoolbooks and homework.

John: It's my life.

Suzie: You're right. And maybe it's OK for you.

Valerie: But don't you ever—?

John: Yeah! Sure, I want to have fun. Sure I'd like to go to games and parties and maybe even dances. But I can't do that. Don't you understand? I can't afford to let up. And it's going to be worth it...in the long run. At least that's what my mom and dad say.

Mr. Hoskins: Do I detect a note of regret there?

John: (*Looking at* **Mr. Hoskins**) I've got to get good grades. There's a lot of pressure on me. But I can't disappoint my folks, can I?

Questions for Discussion

1. How does Mike apply peer pressure to John?

2. Do your friends pressure you to do things you don't want to do? If so, how do you deal with it?

3. Is John effective in how he handles Mike's pressure?

4. Discuss dating customs in your locality. Do you agree or disagree with them?

5. In what ways are dating customs different now than in your parents' generation?

6. Do you agree or disagree with John about studying? Why?

DEATH AND DYING

Grandparents Shouldn't Die

*The action occurs in a classroom just before the
start of a math class.
Margot is sitting at her desk, crying
as the other students enter one by one.*

Jessica: (*Rushing toward her*) Margot, what's wrong? Did something happen?

> **David** *and* **Charles** *enter and take their seats,
> followed by* **Johanna.**

Margot: It's my grandma.

David: Is she ill?

Margot: She's in the hospital, in intensive care.

Jessica: Oh, Margot, I'm sorry.

Margot: But you don't understand. She's not expected to live.

David: My grandfather died last summer. I know how you feel.

Margot: It's not fair. Grandparents aren't supposed to die. Not for a long time. I love her too much to lose her.

Mrs. McFarland enters and crosses to her desk in the front of the room.

Mrs. McFarland: All right, class... Margot, are you all right?

Margot: (*Shakes her head*) It's my grandma.

Johanna: Her grandmother's in the hospital.

Mrs. McFarland: I'm sorry.

Margot: I love her so much. I just can't stand to lose her.

Mrs. McFarland: (*Sighing*) I wish there was a way to help, Margot. Do you want to talk about it?

Margot: She has cancer; we didn't know, and it's gotten really bad.

Johanna: Do you mean she didn't tell you?

Margot: No, she didn't know either. Then she passed out, and they rushed her to the hospital. It started in her lymph glands and...

David: Lymphoma. I know about that. That's how my grandpa died too.

Mrs. McFarland: (*To* **David**) I'm sorry. (*To* **Margot**) I'm sure she knows you love her.

Margot: But I don't want her to die. She's a really important person in my life. I love her as much as I love my parents.

Johanna: My mom died...when I was only five. Sometimes I think I don't even remember her.

Mrs. McFarland: Not remembering is understandable. Five is a young age.

Johanna: It made me decide I want to be a doctor, or work in medicine in some other way. Maybe I can help prevent the same kind of thing happening to other kids.

Margot: I couldn't stand to lose my mom. I don't know what I'd do.

Mrs. McFarland: Let's delay our math lesson. I think maybe this is more important to talk about now.

Charles: Have you been to see your grandma?

Margot: Mom wasn't sure I should.

Charles: My uncle got killed. A couple of years ago. He was riding his motorcycle and got hit by a car. There was a whole court thing about it. The driver of the car went to jail, but now he's out. Uncle Bob didn't die right away. He was in the hospital for a couple of days. The hospital wouldn't let me see him. I was too young, so I never got to tell him goodbye.

Johanna: I didn't tell my mom goodbye either. I didn't even know she was dying; nobody bothered to tell me.

David: Death is something we have to accept, I guess. At least that's what Dad says. That dying's a part of life.

Charles: Not a part most of us want to think about. I know I don't.

David: Me either. It's like it happens to other people; it'll never happen to us.

Margot: Maybe not to us personally, but to people we love.

Mrs. McFarland: As David said, it's inevitable. Something we all have to face. Something we have to accept.

Margot: My grandma's not so old. Her own mother's still alive. In a nursing home.

Mrs. McFarland: It isn't fair, is it? Some people die when they're very young. Some live for many years.

David: Our next door neighbor had a baby that died. He was OK one minute, and the next he was turning blue and couldn't breathe.

Johanna: What happened?

David: I don't know.

Mrs. McFarland: They used to call it crib death. But more and more doctors are thinking it's not all caused by the same thing.

David: I saw a thing on TV about some mattresses in car seats that can smother a baby.

Margot: I think I'll tell my mom that I want to go see my grandma. I want to say goodbye. I'm going to miss her so much.

Johanna: I remember how much I missed my mom.

David: And how I missed my grandpa. We used to go fishing together.

Margot: (*Trying to smile*) Grandma and I always went to the park. Sometimes to the zoo; sometimes just for a picnic. Just her and me. It was really special.

Mrs. McFarland: All we can do is hang on to the memories. They're among the most precious things we have.

David: But we forget. After a time we forget. I know. (*He turns to* **Johanna.**) You said you have trouble sometimes remembering your mom. Sometimes I can't even remember what my grandpa looked like.

Johanna: But I was just a little girl when she died. Now I'd remember.

Charles: When I was a little kid, I remember telling my mom that I wanted us all to die at the same time—her and dad and my grandparents and me.

Mrs. McFarland: Then you wouldn't be sad, would you? (**Charles** *shakes his head.*) But you'd miss out on so much too.

Charles: I used to feel that way, but I don't anymore. Well, sometimes I do.

Mrs. McFarland: Has any of this helped, Margot?

Margot: I think so. But she's still going to die. And there's nothing we can do to stop it.

Questions for Discussion

1. Why is being able to talk about death and dying import-ant?

2. Has someone close to you died? Would you like to tell the class about it?

3. David says, "My grandfather died last summer. I know how you feel." Do you think he does know how Mar-got is feeling? Is this usually an appropriate response?

4. Mrs. McFarland puts her lesson plans aside to allow the class to discuss an issue that is very important to Mar-got. Should she have done this? Why or why not?

5. Do you think your parents should shield you from the reality of death until you get older? Would you rather they make the decision for you about visiting a dying grandparent so you would not have to make that deci-sion for yourself, and thus not feel guilty about not going to the hospital?

6. What are some feelings a person might have when he or she has not been able to say goodbye to a dying per-son?

Popular Student Dies in An Accident

*The action takes place before a social studies class. The teacher, **Mr. Moore,** has agreed to meet with some of Peter Douglas' friends to talk about his death. As the action begins, the students are settling into their seats. **Mr. Moore** is sitting on the front of his desk.*

Mr. Moore: I know we agreed to talk about the terrible thing that happened to Peter Douglas. So we'll concentrate on that. Maybe it can help to air our feelings, to see that each of us isn't alone in missing him.

Gary: I just can't believe it happened.

Mr. Moore: You and he were best friends.

Gary: Since he moved here almost four years ago. I remember it really well. He was walking down the sidewalk like he was lost. "Hey, kid," I said. "You looking for someone?" He came over and we started to talk, and pretty soon we were spending all our free time together.

Mr. Moore: It must be especially rough on you.

Gary: We walked to school together yesterday like we always do—like we always did. And then Mom picked me up after my last class for a dentist's appointment. If I hadn't gone to get my tooth filled, maybe Peter wouldn't... Maybe if I'd been with him, he'd still be alive.

Shauna: It wasn't your fault. You shouldn't blame yourself.

Gary: I guess so, but I can't help it.

Betsy: I'm going to miss him too. We were working on this project. Well, you know, Mr. Moore. It was this report and building a model... I was glad I was getting to know him.

Shauna: He went to my church. We were in the same Sunday School class. It won't be the same.

Billy: Why didn't he see the car? Couldn't he get out of the way?

Mr. Moore: I'm sure we'll never know that, Billy. And think of the poor driver who hit him. What he must feel like because of it.

Gary: Man! He was always so careful. I even used to tease him about how careful he was. If a car was two blocks away, he'd wait till it passed before he crossed the street.

Tricia: How did it happen, does anyone know? I didn't hear anything about it till I got to school today.

Gary: He ran out in front of a car, that's all I heard. The driver didn't have time to stop. Man, it doesn't seem fair. He was younger than I am. Almost a whole year younger... It's like it's all a bad dream. Mom'll wake me up and tell me Peter's downstairs waiting for me. And I'll get dressed real quick, and grab some breakfast, and we'll start out for school. (*Fighting a lump in his throat*) Except that he's dead.

Betsy: Maybe God wanted him, needed him in heaven. That's what Daddy said when my Grandpa died.

Tricia: Why would God be so mean?

Shauna: We can't understand that kind of thing.

Mr. Moore: Anything else?

Jerry: Well, I know I'm going to miss him too. Even if I didn't know him very well. (*He turns to* **Gary.**) I know you and he were best friends. But the rest of us liked him too. He was one of the most popular kids in school.

Billy: He was always trying to help someone. He helped me a lot when I was having trouble with math. I was lost when we first got into that stuff about algebra.

Tricia: And he did other things too. Other nice things, I mean. Like always trying to break up fights.

Gary: My grandma always used to say the good die young. So I guess it's true.

Mr. Moore: It may seem that way, Gary. And it certainly is in this case. But death is no respecter of persons. (*He smiles faintly.*) That's an old saying too. And I suspect there's more truth in that one. No one's immune from death.

Gary: You mean we're all going to die. I know that. But not for years. Not for a long, long time. It makes me angry what happened to Peter, you know?

Mr. Moore: It makes me angry too. Maybe even a little angry at Peter for getting himself killed.

Tricia: You mean he should have been more careful.

Mr. Moore: You're darned right he should have. Everyone should be more careful and not have to die. Do you hear what I'm saying? I'm angry, and maybe so are you. But that's natural. It's like people leave us here on our own without them. It's like they're deserting us.

Gary: I didn't want to say that.

Mr. Moore: It's OK, Gary, you don't have to say it, because I did.

Gary: Even though I miss him, I guess I feel that way a little bit too. "Darn it, Peter," I'd like to tell him, "why didn't you be a little more careful? Like you always were before."

Betsy: It's like when anyone dies. The surprise...the shock hasn't even worn off.

Tricia: And when it does, we're going to miss him more, is that what you mean?

Betsy: Yes. It's like we'll look up and expect him to come through the door. And he won't be there. And his seat will be empty.

Gary: My whole life is going to be empty. (*He shakes his head.*) I guess that sounds pretty selfish. Thinking about me instead of Peter.

Billy: Maybe you have the right to be selfish. We all do. He's gone, and we're here without him.

Gary: It's going to be so different without him. We hung out every weekend. Went to a Saturday matinee or down to the playground to see if we could get a game started. He loved baseball. I like it too, but not as much as Peter did. He never wanted to miss a game on TV, and he could quote all the stats.

Billy: I know. It was amazing. What was a player's RBI. Any player's RBI. Pete could tell you. I don't know how he remembered it all.

Mr. Moore: We'll have to stop. It's nearly time for the bell. Has any of this helped?

Gary: It doesn't bring Peter back.

Mr. Moore: No, it doesn't do that.

Betsy: But maybe it helps me accept a little better what happened.

Mr. Moore: Good.

Questions for Discussion

1. Why does Gary feel it is his fault that Peter died? Have you known of other incidences when someone has felt the same way?

2. Gary says, "I just can't believe that it happened." Later he says that he is angry at Peter for getting himself killed. Denial and anger are two of the five steps Elizabeth Kubler-Ross talks about in her book, *On Death and Dying*. What are the other three steps?

3. Being a good listener is one way you can help a friend who has lost someone close. What are some other things you can do to help a friend who is grieving?

4. Gary and Peter were very good friends, but the others in the class knew and liked Peter too. Do you think Gary felt a deeper loss than the others, or did all of the classmates have similar feelings?

DECISION MAKING

But What Can We Do?

The action takes place at Ashley's house,
where several people have gathered to talk about
one of their teachers.

Ashley: I don't know if it's going to do any good to talk about this.

Luke: What do you mean?

Ashley: Well, how's it going to help? We can discuss it, but what can we really do to solve the problem? We don't have any authority.

Teesa: I'm sick of being put down all the time. Mrs. Richardson wants our respect, so why doesn't she respect us?

Willie: You said it. I don't even think she even knows how to speak in a normal tone of voice. All she can do is yell.

Kim: So what are we going to do?

Teesa: Maybe we could talk to her.

Willie: Oh, yeah, sure. Has any kid you know of ever been able to talk to her?

Ashley: Only to give answers in class.

Kim: Why do you think she treats us that way?

Teesa: I don't know, but there has to be a reason. What do the rest of you think?

Luke: I think we're wasting our time, that's what I think.

Kim: Then why are you here, Luke?

Luke: I don't know. Grasping at straws, I guess. I mean, how many more times do you want to have tests without any warning or so much homework on weekends you can hardly get it done?

Teesa: If she were just starting out teaching, I could understand. But she's been teaching for years. My uncle even had her.

Kim: I don't follow.

Teesa: Like last year when we had that practice teacher. She made a lot of mistakes, but she admitted it.

Willie: I can't see Mrs. Richardson admitting to doing anything wrong.

Ashley: I don't want to get her fired or anything, but how about talking to the school board?

Luke: You've got to be kidding. Why would they listen to us?

Kim: I've talked to my parents about it; they know how she is. So someone believes us.

Willie: And all the kids who've had her before. They certainly believe it.

Teesa: But you know what? She wasn't always this way.

Luke: What do you mean?

Teesa: Like I said, my uncle had her, and he liked her. He couldn't believe she's changed so much.

Luke: Our Mrs. Richardson? That's who you're talking about?

Teesa: It's true.

Ashley: Even so, that doesn't do anything to solve our problem.

Kim: What if we got together and tried to talk to her? After school some day.

Willie: You can count me out.

Luke: Chicken.

Willie: Yeah, well, maybe I am. But I figure if I get out of her class alive next spring, I'm lucky. I'm not going to rock the boat.

Kim: So what you're saying is that it's OK for her to be like she is, and we should just try to get through it.

Willie: (*Shrugs*) It's only a few more months.

Luke: I for one can't stand the woman.

Willie: So that means you're volunteering to talk to her?

Luke: It doesn't mean any such thing.

Ashley: Look, we're not getting anywhere by arguing with each other.

Teesa: What if we talked to the principal?

Kim: Do you really think he'd listen?

Teesa: I think he might. He must have heard about some of the things she does—her attitude. It's like she hates kids. I mean I don't enjoy being yelled at in front of the class and made fun of like...like I don't have any feelings.

Luke: I know what you mean. And she acts like she knows everything...like she's so much better than we are.

Teesa: I still think there has to be a reason. Maybe she's sick...or having some kind of problems at home.

Willie: That doesn't give her the right to treat us the way she does.

Teesa: No, it doesn't. But maybe if she knew we sympathized with her. I mean if something really is wrong.

Luke: It would take a lot for me to sympathize with her.

Ashley: Well, I don't think we're going to get anything settled.

Kim: I'm afraid you're right.

Willie: You mean we're just going to let her go on like she is.

Luke: Like I said, the best thing to do is try to ignore it.

Kim: Well, I don't agree with that at all.

Luke: But you don't have any answers; there's nothing anyone can come up with that we can do.

Teesa: What if we tried to treat her better?

Willie: Sure! Just what I want to do. Hey, Mrs. Richardson, I'm glad you yelled at me. And to show you how happy I am, I'm going to treat you especially nice.

Ashley: Darn it, Willie, that kind of thing doesn't help.

Willie: I'm sorry. Now I'm sounding just like her.

Ashley: Maybe Teesa's idea's the best.

Kim: But what if it doesn't work?

Luke: That's right. What if it doesn't work? Then we're no better off than we are now.

Ashley: But at least we'd have tried.

Questions for Discussion

1. The students want to decide what to do about Mrs. Richardson's behavior toward them. What are some of the things they suggest doing?

2. What other things might they have suggested?

3. Teesa says her uncle had Mrs. Richardson as a teacher and he liked her. Why do you think Mrs. Richardson changed so much over the years? Or did the students change?

4. What decision does the group make? Do you think it will work?

5. Ashley says, "But at least we'd have tried." Do you think it is better to try and not succeed, or to decide to not try at all?

Are Grades Worth It?

The action takes place in the cafeteria.
Henry, Frank *and* **Randy** *are eating lunch.*

Randy: I don't know how you do it, Henry.

Henry: What do you mean?

Randy: How you do so well in all your classes. I never see you studying.

Henry: My superior brain. Something mere earthlings wouldn't understand.

Randy: Yeah, sure.

Frank: Randy's right. You're tops in all your classes. I don't know how you do it either.

Henry: (*Turning to face them*) OK, I'll tell you. But you have to promise me something.

Frank: Yeah? What is it?

Henry: I mean it. You have to promise.

Randy: You sound pretty serious, Henry.

Henry: I am serious.

Randy: What's going on anyhow?

Henry: You promise?

Randy: I guess so.

Henry: How about you, Frank?

Frank: If you say so.

Henry: OK, man, I'm holding you to it.

Frank: So come on, give. What's your big, dark secret?

Henry: It's easy to get good grades if you know the right people.

Randy: The right people? I don't understand.

Frank: I think I do. You're getting the answers from somewhere, aren't you?

Henry: So what if I am?

Frank: Are you?

Henry: Well, you know that kid who sits in the corner all by himself?

Randy: What kid?

Henry: You know; the one who's always studying.

Frank: Yeah, Mel Smith. What about him?

Henry: Did you ever see such a...such a total loser before?

Randy: Come on, Henry. What about this kid?

Henry: He does my homework for me. Or at least he lets me "borrow" his.

Frank: What!

Henry: Yeah, that's right. All I have to do is pay off. He studies all the time, never has any money. Look at what he wears if you want to know that.

Randy: You pay this kid?

Henry: Kind of. I buy things for him. Tapes and CDs of his favorite groups. That's all there is to it. Pretty easy, huh?

Frank: What if you get caught?

Henry: Now how would I get caught? I copy what he does. And we're both smart enough to change the answers at least a little bit. So his and mine won't be exactly the same.

Randy: You know, Henry, that really surprises me. I didn't think you'd do stuff like that.

Henry: Hey, man, why not? You know how my parents are. Pushing me for grades. Well, I found a way to make everyone happy. My parents, me, and the kid who gets his CDs.

Frank: That's still only the homework.

Henry: You mean the tests?

Frank: Yeah.

Henry: You notice where I sit, don't you?

Randy: You used to sit near the front.

Henry: Right. So now I sit next to Melvin Smith. I keep an eye on everything he does, if you know what I mean.

Frank: You mean you copy his tests as well? Geez, Henry, grades can't be that important.

Henry: Not to me they aren't. But you don't know my parents very well.

Randy: What do you mean?

Henry: They were always on me about how I was never as good as they were in school because I don't try. So they both got good grades, so what? I guess I just didn't inherit their talent. But like I said, the problem's solved.

Frank: I don't think you should be doing this. What if you get caught?

Henry: Not a chance. And you both promised, right? You're not going to tell. So what's the big deal? I have it made. Maybe Mel will do your homework too.

Frank: No, thanks.

Henry: It's up to you. (*He stands and walks away.*)

Randy: Man, do you believe that?

Frank: Come on, Randy, let's go to class.

Randy: We're just going to let him get away with it? I don't like that. I work hard for my grades. Well, maybe not as hard as my folks would like.

Frank: I'm not going to be a snitch, are you?

Randy: I still don't like it.

Frank: Well, neither did I. But we did make a promise. And if we break it, we're just as bad as Henry is.

Randy: I guess so. But if he lies and cheats, why can't we?

Frank: Are you going to be the one to tell?

Randy: (*Picks up his tray, turns and starts to walk away*) I guess not.

Frank: Well, neither am I.

Questions for Discussion

1. Henry made a decision to cheat. What may be some of the long-term consequences of his decision?

2. Do you think Mel is aware that he also is making a decision to cheat?

3. Henry says that he must make good grades because of his parents' expectations. Do you think he would have cheated if his parents had not put so much pressure on him to succeed?

4. Do you think Randy and Frank should report Henry for cheating? Why or why not?

5. Decisions are often made based on one's values. According to the decisions Henry made, what do you think

are his most important values? What are his least important ones?

DISHONESTY

Little White Lies

*The action takes place at a city park just after a
basketball game.*

Erica: I'm sorry you can't come over to my house, Garth. I
was looking forward to playing my new tapes for you.

Garth: I know, but my mom says I have to mow the yard
and help her with the garden. There's nothing I can do
to get out of it.

Erica: I understand. Maybe tomorrow?

Garth: I'll try. But I'm not so sure. It depends if I get everything done and we don't go to my grandparents'
house.

Erica: OK, goodbye, you two.

Joel: See you Monday.

Erica: Yeah, sure, school. Did you have to remind me? One
more week till vacation.

Joel: I thought girls were supposed to like school.

Erica: Not this girl.

Joel: (*Grins*) Sorry.

Erica: Well, let me know, Garth. I know you've been wanting to hear those tapes. (*She exits.*)

Garth: Sure thing, Erica.

Joel: I didn't know you had to help your mother.

Garth: Are you serious? I don't have to do much of anything if I don't want to.

Joel: I don't understand.

Garth: No big deal. So how'd you like to take in a movie? I hear that the Stephen King film at the mall is pretty good.

Joel: But you told Erica—

Garth: What's the difference what I told Erica?

Joel: You lied to her? Why?

Garth: I just didn't want to go to her house, that's all. Why should I go if I don't really want to?

Joel: Why did you tell her you would?

Garth: It was easy, that's all. No harm. You know she likes me. I thought I'd make her feel good by telling her I'd stop over tomorrow.

Joel: I can't believe you'd do something like that.

Garth: What's it to you?

Joel: You're my friend, that's what. And I thought I knew you pretty well.

Garth: If you're my friend, just leave it be.

Joel: It's like your telling my Mom you got that new bike. Fifteen hundred dollars, for gosh sake. Why'd you even say such a thing?

Garth: It sounded good at the time.

Joel: Yeah?

Garth: I don't lie about things that really matter. So what's the problem?

Joel: I don't see any reason to do it, that's all.

Garth: Oh, in your whole life, you've never told a lie, right?

Joel: I didn't say that.

Garth: People lie all the time. Like telling people what you know they want to hear.

Joel: What do you mean?

Garth: Like your mom gets a new dress, and it's dumb-looking? Do you tell her that? Does your father tell her?

Joel: What, are you crazy?

Garth: So in other words you lie.

Joel: Well, maybe I stretch the truth.

Garth: So how's that any different from what I do?

Joel: You make up all kinds of things. Things that are silly. Like the bike.

Garth: You mean it's wrong to lie about the bike, but it's OK to lie about your mom's new dress.

Joel: That isn't what I said.

Garth: Isn't it?

Joel: It's just that...I wouldn't want to hurt Mom's feelings.

Garth: Just like I didn't want to hurt Erica's. And I would've if I'd told her I just didn't want to hear her stupid tapes.

Joel: You're getting me mixed up.

Garth: Am I?

Joel: Yeah, you are.

Garth: Good. So come on. Let's see when the movie starts.

Questions for Discussion

1. Do you think Garth should have told Erica that he didn't want to go to her house? Why or why not?

2. Joel reminds Garth that he has been dishonest about going to Erica's house and also about the price of a bike. Do you think people who are dishonest about one thing will be dishonest about other things? Why or why not?

3. Joel seems to disapprove of Garth's lying. What could he do to help Garth learn to be truthful?

4. Joel says, "Well, maybe I stretch the truth." What is the difference between stretching the truth and lying?

5. Joel says, "You are getting me mixed up." Do you think it is Garth's intentions to confuse Joel? Why or why not?

6. Do you feel that Garth really believes he is lying? Have you known people who lied but did not believe they were doing it?

Shoplifting

The action takes place outside a large department store at a mall.

Keith: (*Pulling a cigarette lighter out of his pocket*) See what I got, man?

Ed: Where'd you get that?

Keith: In the store, where do you think?

Robin: I didn't see you buy it.

Keith: Why would I buy something like this? I don't smoke.

Robin: You stole it?

Keith: Yeah, so what?

Ed: Why'd you do that? You're just going to get into trouble.

The store's manager, **Mrs. Fairfield,** *rushes out of the store toward them.*

Mrs. Fairfield: I've got you now. You've stolen one thing too many.

> **Mr. Simmons,** *the store detective, comes up behind them.*

Keith: (*Turning to run*) Come on, let's go. Let's go.

Mr. Simmons: (*Grabbing him*) Not so fast, young man. You're not going anywhere.

Keith: What did I do?

Mrs. Fairfield: For starters, you stole the lighter you're holding. You also took a wallet and a key chain.

Keith: OK, so you caught me. What are you going to do? (*He reaches into his pocket and takes out a wallet and key chain.*)

Mrs. Fairfield: What I'm going to do, young man, is call the police. They can deal with you. (*She looks at the others.*) So far as you two are concerned, I'm calling your folks, just so they'll know the sort of company you're keeping.

Robin: We didn't do anything. We didn't know he was going to take those things.

Ed: She's right. If you call my folks, I'm going to be in big trouble. You can search me, if you like. I didn't take anything.

Mr. Simmons: Maybe they're right. (*He turns to them.*) I was keeping an eye on the three of you, and I know you didn't even see your friend pick up the three things he stole. (*He looks at* **Keith.**) You were pretty slick, sliding them into your pocket. But not slick enough.

Robin: Can't we just leave? I'm going to be in big trouble with my folks. And it isn't my fault. Mine or Ed's.

Keith: Can't I give the stuff back? I promise not to do it again.

Mrs. Fairfield: This isn't the first time, is it? (*She waits.*) Well, is it?

Keith: (*Quietly*) No.

Mrs. Fairfield: What did you say?

Keith: I said it wasn't the first time.

Mrs. Fairfield: I think you'd better all come inside. I'm going to let you off easy. I'll call your folks to come and get you. But I better never see you again in this store.

Scene ii

The actions occurs in a lounge inside the store.
Robin, Ed *and* **Keith** *are sitting by themselves.*

Robin: Why did you take those things?

Ed: Why did you even want them? The wallet maybe, but not the other stuff.

Keith: I don't want them.

Ed: Then why did you take them?

Keith: Just to see if I could.

Robin: Have you done this before, like Mrs. Fairfield said?

Keith: Taken things?

Ed: Yeah. How many times?

Keith: I don't know. Ten? Fifteen?

Robin: Why, for heaven's sake?

Keith: I told you. It's fun. It's scary. I don't know.

Robin: And so you got us all in trouble.

Keith: Just me, not you.

Ed: They're calling our folks to come and get us. If that isn't trouble, I don't know what is.

Robin: I still don't understand why you take things you don't even want. Do you sell them or something?

Keith: Nah.

Ed: What then?

Keith: I toss them.

Ed: Man, I think you're one messed up kid.

Keith: What's it to you anyhow?

Ed: Well, I'll tell you what. Because of you, I'm in trouble. I didn't even want to go into that store. But you did. And now I'm going to have to pay for it. My parents are going to want to know why this happened. And what am I supposed to tell them?

Robin: I'll bet I won't even be allowed to come to the mall by myself anymore.

Keith: Come on, you two. It's not a big thing. I told you I do it all the time. Plenty of other kids do too.

Robin: So I guess that makes it all right.

Keith: I don't believe you two. So I took some stuff, and I happened to get caught. Next time I'll be a little more careful.

Questions for Discussion

1. Keith says that he doesn't smoke and therefore doesn't need the lighter. Why do you think he stole it?

2. Ed and Robin say they did not know Keith was going to steal from the store. Do you think they are treated fairly by Mrs. Fairfield? Why or why not?

3. Keith does not seem sorry that he has stolen from the store. In fact, he says, "Next time I'll be a little more careful." Do you think Ed and Robin will remain Keith's friends? Would you?

4. Shoplifters cause everyone to pay more for merchandise because the store owner must raise prices to cover his or her losses. What do you think can be done to stop shoplifting?

DIVORCE

Daughter Is the Victim

Scene i

*The action takes place in the living room of the house where **Stacy** lives with her mother and four-year-old brother.*

Mrs. Doyle: I told you to clean up your mess, and I mean it.

Stacy: Mooom!

Mrs. Doyle: I don't know what I'm going to do with you. Ever since the divorce, you've acted like a spoiled little brat.

Stacy: (*Starts to exit*) I'm going to my room to study.

Mrs. Doyle: Come back here, Stacy. And I mean right now. I don't have to put up with this kind of behavior.

Stacy: What did I do? I don't even know what you mean.

Mrs. Doyle: I told you to straighten up this room. You're the one who left it in such a mess.

Stacy: (*Picks up a magazine from the floor and places it on the coffee table*) There, are you happy?

Mrs. Doyle: Don't talk back to me. I won't put up with it, do you hear me?

Stacy: All right, Mom, I'm sorry.

Mrs. Doyle: Until you learn to behave, you're restricted to your room.

Stacy: (*Unbelieving*) I don't know what you mean. What did I do?

Mrs. Doyle: It's your attitude, the way you act. That's what I mean.

Stacy: OK, Mom, whatever you say.

Scene ii

The action takes place at the end of the school day. **Stacy** *and* **Cassie** *have stopped to talk before walking home in opposite directions.*

Stacy: I'm telling you, Cassie, it's gotten completely crazy.

Cassie: That bad, huh?

Stacy: You don't know the half of it.

Cassie: I'll be glad to listen.

Stacy: Mom is frustrated, I know that. She didn't want the divorce. Dad did. But maybe it's better than their fight-

103

ing all the time. I don't know, but that's beside the point.

Cassie: What is the point, Stacy?

Stacy: Mom's taking it out on me. I can't do anything right, no matter what.

Cassie: All because of the divorce.

Stacy: Yes. Last night she restricted me to my room for the whole week. Because of my attitude, she says.

Cassie: You didn't do anything?

Stacy: She says I didn't straighten up the living room like she asked. But I did. I dusted and vacuumed. But do you know what upset her?

Cassie: What?

Stacy: I was looking at one of her magazines—*National Geographic* or something—and I didn't put it back on the coffee table.

Cassie: That's it?

Stacy: That's it. It's not my fault Dad left. But you'd certainly think it was if you saw the way Mom is acting.

Cassie: What can you do about it?

Stacy: At this stage, I don't know. I can't even talk to her or she'll snap off my head.

Cassie: Do you think things will get better? That she won't take it out on you so much?

Stacy: I don't know. Dad's gone for good, I'm sure of that. We talked it out, all three of us.

Cassie: I guess you just have to wait it out, huh? And hope that things get better.

Questions for Discussion

1. Do you think Stacy could have said or done anything differently that would have kept her from being restricted? If so, what?

2. Who do you think suffers the most in a divorce, the parent or the child?

3. Cassie says, "I guess you just have to wait it out, huh? And hope that things get better." Do you think this is what Stacy should do? Why or why not?

4. Talk about other ways divorce affects the family.

Relationship Is Not Destroyed

The action occurs in the Keefers' living room.

Scott: So you're just going to leave, and that's that?

Dad: Of course not, Scott. We'll keep in touch.

Scott: Sure, just like Bob and I keep in touch since he moved away.

Dad: It's not the same thing. I'm your father. I love you.

Scott: Then why are you leaving?

Dad: You know why, Scott. Things just aren't working out for your Mom and me.

Scott: But why do you have to go so far away? I looked it up on the map, and you'll be way on the other side of the country.

Dad: We'll talk on the phone, at least a couple of times a week. More often if we want to.

Scott: I'm afraid you won't want to, Dad.

Dad: Oh, Scottie, you know how I feel about you.

Scott: I thought I knew how you felt about Mom too. And how she felt about you.

Dad: It's not the same thing. You're my son; you'll always be my son.

Scott: I'll never get to see you.

Dad: Sure, you will.

Scott: I'm going to miss you. I'll really miss you.

Dad: (*Throwing his arms around* **Scott**) I'll miss you too. You know that. (*Breaking the embrace*) Look, Scott, it's for the best. You know things weren't good between your mom and me. And when my company offered me the chance to set up a division in New England, I thought it was the best solution.

Scott: OK.

Dad: You sure?

Scott: I guess so.

Scene ii

The action occurs two months later at the Polski's, where **Scott** *and his friend* **Rick** *are talking in Rick's room.*

Scott: So anyhow when my dad called last night—

Rick: You talked to him?

Scott: Yeah, sure. He calls every Wednesday and Saturday. And sometimes more than that.

Rick: You told me you were worried about that. That you thought you'd lose touch with him.

Scott: I know. But it's not like that at all. And I'm going to go see him when school's out.

Rick: That's great. I almost never hear from my mom. Not since she got married again.

Scott: That's too bad, Rick.

Rick: Well, it's been a long time. Four or five years, I guess. I'm getting used to it.

Scott: (*Worried*) Did she keep in touch at first?

Rick: Not really. Not like your dad.

Scott: I guess I didn't have to worry. Things worked out OK. (*Smiles*) I guess I should have known.

Questions for Discussion

1. Do you think Scott or Rick's situation with his parent is the most typical?

2. Scott was afraid that he would lose contact with his father. Are you surprised that he does not?

3. Rick says that he was getting used to not seeing his mother. Do you think he really means it? Why or why not?

4. Is there anything that Rick can do to change his situation with his mother? If so, what?

Whom to Live With?

The action takes place at a fast food restaurant.
Lee, George, Betty, *and* **Syble** *are sitting at a booth and eating.*

Lee: When did you find out, George?

George: Just last night. Mom and Dad called us all together and told us at the same time.

Betty: That must be hard to hear. I mean...that your parents are splitting up.

George: I couldn't believe it. I knew things hadn't been going well, especially since Dad lost his job. But I didn't think they were even considering a divorce.

Syble: Two years ago I couldn't believe it either. But I do now. My parents are definitely divorced!

Betty: I remember when you first heard. You came over to my house, and you couldn't stop crying.

George: I remember how sad you seemed for days at school. I felt sorry for you. (*Pause*) I guess I thought then that a divorce is something that happens to someone else's family. I never dreamed it would happen to mine.

Syble: I'd always thought the same thing.

Lee: I guess it can happen to any of us.

Syble: But life does go on. (*Laughs*) I'm still here. I didn't die after all, even if I did feel like it at times.

George: But I don't know if I'll still be here or not.

Syble: (*Shocked*) What are you saying?

George: I just mean I may move away with my dad. If I do, I won't be here next year.

Betty: Well, that's a relief. (*The others look at her.*) I mean, I'm glad you aren't going to die. I thought you were talking about suicide.

George: No, nothing like that. I asked Dad last night where he was going with his suitcase. He said just to a friend's house, but he'd soon be going out of state to look for work.

Betty: Do you want to go with him?

George: Not really. I mean I'd like to be with him, but I don't want to leave all my friends.

Lee: Then why are you thinking about leaving?

George: Because Dad will be all alone. The girls are going to stay in the house with Mom, of course. If I don't move with him, he won't have anyone.

Betty: Has he asked you to go?

George: No, he wouldn't do that. He wouldn't want to take me away from school and my friends. I'll have to convince him that I really want to go.

Betty: But what about the rest of your family? Won't you miss your mom and your sisters?

George: Sure I will. But they will have each other. (*Smiling*) Besides, who wants to be in a house with only women?

Lee: I'd think about this real seriously, George. I mean, before I did anything.

Syble: That's right, George. You probably aren't even used to the idea that your parents are divorcing.

Questions for Discussion

1. How do you think George felt when his parents told him they were getting a divorce? Can you relate to his situation?

2. George has three friends to talk to about his problem. Discuss what it might have been like if he didn't have friends. Who else could he have talked to?

3. Is George being realistic when he talks about moving with his dad? Why or why not?

4. How do you think George may feel if his dad tells him he can't move with him?

5. Do you think George will remain in contact with his dad if he doesn't move? Will he remain close to his mother and sisters if he does move?

DRUGS

The Availability of Drugs

Scene i

*The action takes place in the corridor at Adams School. It's Wendy's first day there after leaving her old school. She's trying to figure out the combination to open her locker when **Lori** comes up to her.*

Lori: Hi, you new here?

Wendy: Oh, yeah, hi. My name's Wendy.

Lori: I'm Lori, in Mrs. Simpson's homeroom.

Wendy: Me too.

Lori: Well, good. Hey, I got some stuff you might want, you know?

Wendy: (*Puzzled*) Stuff? What do you mean?

Lori: Hey, don't you know the score? I'm talking about weed, grass—for starters.

Wendy: (*Shocked*) You mean marijuana?

Lori: Where are you from anyway, Mars or the moon or something?

Wendy: I just didn't understand—

Lori: Listen, that's OK. (*Pause*) So do you want some? I'll tell you what. Out of the goodness of my heart, I'll give you a joint just to show it's good—

Wendy: (*Grabbing things from her locker*) No, thanks.

Lori: Hey, listen, I got some harder stuff too. You like crack? No problem.

Wendy: (*Not knowing what to say*) I...I...

Lori: Well, you think about it. Anytime you're interested, you know where to find me.

Wendy: Thanks, but I don't—

Lori: Once upon a time I didn't either. But that's all changed now. So I'll see you. (*She turns and hurries down the corridor as* **Wendy** *stares after her, still shocked and upset.*)

Scene ii

The action takes place in the Novaks' living room. **Mr. Novak** *is hanging a picture on the wall when* **Wendy** *enters.*

Mr. Novak: Hi, how was your day? How's the new school?

Wendy: (*Her voice flat*) OK, I guess.

Mr. Novak: (*Turning to her*) That doesn't sound so good. Did something go wrong? Did you have trouble with your classes?

Wendy: No, they were fine. About the same as before.

Mr. Novak: Well, something doesn't seem right. Do you want to talk about it? I'm a good listener.

Wendy: (*Trying to smile*) I know that, Daddy.

Mr. Novak: So what is it?

Wendy: Oh, Daddy, everything's different.

Mr. Novak: But I thought you said—

Wendy: I don't know what to do.

Mr. Novak: Come on, honey, let's sit down and talk about it. OK? (*He sits on the sofa and pats the cushion beside him.*)

Wendy: (*Sitting beside him*) All right.

Mr. Novak: So what went wrong?

Wendy: Two different kids came up to me and tried to sell me drugs.

Mr. Novak: I was worried about that.

Wendy: What do you mean?

Mr. Novak: Adams is a big school. This is a big city, a lot different from where we used to live.

Wendy: What's that got to do with it?

Mr. Novak: There's bound to be a drug problem, almost everywhere you go. You read about it in the papers and worry about it.

Wendy: But there wasn't anything like that at Thompsonville. At least, no one offered it to me in the halls.

Mr. Novak: I know. I had my doubts about moving. But when your mom and I both got better jobs...We just couldn't turn them down.

Wendy: I'm afraid, Daddy.

Mr. Novak: Afraid? I don't understand.

Wendy: That I'm not going to be accepted, that nobody's going to like me. I don't want to take drugs, Dad.

Mr. Novak: I never thought you would.

Wendy: But everyone seems to be doing it, and I just won't fit in. There's going to be a lot of pressure, I know. Just like when Jimmy tried to get me to drink at that party before we moved.

Mr. Novak: But you didn't.

Wendy: No, but that was in Thompsonville. Here it seems like everyone's on drugs. Marijuana and crack—

Mr. Novak: I know this is rough, Wendy. But I'm sure not everyone takes drugs.

Wendy: How do you know that? I don't want to be all by myself, without any friends. You know I had a lot of friends before we moved.

Mr. Novak: I know, sweetheart. And I don't know what to tell you. I wish I did.

Wendy: I'm not going to like it here, Dad. I wish we'd move back home. I know we can't, but I wish we could.

Questions for Discussion

1. Do you think that it is realistic for a new girl to be offered drugs on her first day at a new school?

2. Wendy says she wants to be accepted at her new school, but she doesn't want to take drugs. What are some things she can do to accomplish her goal?

3. Mr. Novak says that he doesn't know what to tell Wendy. What would you want your parent to tell you under the same circumstances?

4. Wendy says she would like to move back to her former school. Do you think she will be able to resist the peer pressure to do drugs at her new school? Why or why not?

Parents Using Drugs

*The action takes place in Mrs. Slawson's
social studies class.*

Mrs. Slawson: So just how widespread do you think the
use of drugs is?

Paige: Well, a lot more than most parents think.

Mrs. Slawson: What percentage, do you think?

Paige: That's hard to say. A third maybe? I don't know.

Mrs. Slawson: I'd say at least a third have tried them,
wouldn't you?

Wayne: A lot of kids just want to experiment, I know that.

Mrs. Slawson: You mean they don't use them regularly?

Wayne: I guess not. Most of my friends don't. (*He glances
quickly at* **Steven.**) At least most of them don't.

Anna: My dad would kill me if I tried. I'm only second generation American. Dad says he's worked too hard to make things good to have any of his kids throw it all away.

Mrs. Slawson: Why do you think kids do drugs?

Paige: A lot of reasons, I guess. To see what it's like. To escape problems.

Wayne: Because they can't help it.

Mrs. Slawson: Why do you say that, Wayne?

Wayne: Because they're available, that's what I mean.

Mrs. Slawson: Peer pressure?

Wayne: Well, yeah, but...

Mrs. Slawson: Go ahead, Wayne, we're interested in what you were going to say.

Wayne: It's nothing.

Mrs. Slawson: (*Smiling*) Okay, another time. (*To the rest of the class*) So what kind of drugs do kids use here in school, do you think?

Alan: Well, weed for one thing. That's pretty much available to everyone. I mean kids come up to me all the time and ask me if I want to buy it.

Anna: And crack. It seems like a lot of kids have at least tried crack.

Mrs. Slawson: A pretty dangerous thing to try. So what do you think we can do about all this?

Anna: It has to start with the parents, just like—

Steven: That's for sure.

Wayne: I think if people stop looking at drugs as something you have to do. As something...

Mrs. Slawson: Glamorous, maybe?

Wayne: Right.

Alan: And if the principal and everyone came down harder on users.

The bell rings signaling the end of class.

Mrs. Slawson: OK, that's it. Remember for tomorrow you're to read chapter thirteen.

Scene ii

*The action takes place at a fast food restaurant after school. **Wayne** and **Steven** have stopped in for a Coke before going home.*

Wayne: So what'd you think about social studies? I mean, I'm surprised that many kids use drugs.

Steven: I'm not. (*Pause*) I smoke weed, you know. I've been doing it now for a couple of years.

Wayne: I know that, Steven. And I've often wondered why. I mean, you do well in school. You're popular.

Steven: Yeah, well, my dad thought it was cute.

Wayne: Your father!

Steven: He and Mom have been smoking weed ever since I can remember. It was always there. Practically every time I walk into the house, I can smell it.

Wayne: I never knew that.

Steven: Yeah, and I hate it. I don't like to have friends over. I know they can tell.

Wayne: What can you do about it? Any idea?

Steven: I want to quit, man. I mean at first it was great to get high.

Wayne: But not anymore?

Steven *shakes his head.*

Wayne: It sounds like you have a real problem. My parents are a lot like Anna said hers are. They'd kill me if I smoked. And if I shot up, man, that would be it. Not that I ever would. I mean, I think it's stupid—Oh, wow, I shouldn't have said that. I'm sorry.

Steven: Well, it is stupid. I mean the first thing everyone does when my parents have friends over is light up. So even if I don't smoke, I get high on what's just floating around in the air.

Wayne: Have you talked to anyone about this?

Steven: You, that's all. Why?

Wayne: How about one of the counselors?

Steven: What could they do? I'd just get my folks in trouble.

Wayne: Maybe you're right.

Steven: Well, I want to quit, and I don't know how. I wish I knew what to do.

Wayne: There's got to be someone you can talk to. Do your parents know how you feel?

Steven: I don't know; I doubt it.

Wayne: Would it do any good to tell them?

Steven: My parents think it's "cool." Can you believe that?

Wayne: Can't you just quit on your own?

Steven: I suppose I can try, 'cause I really don't want to do it.

Questions for Discussion

1. Mrs. Slawson asks the question, "Why do you think kids do drugs?" What would your answer be?

2. Do you think a parent giving a child marijuana should be considered child abuse? Why or why not?

3. Steven says that he wants to quit, but doesn't know how. If he asked you for help, what would you say to him?

4. Wayne says that his parents would kill him if he used drugs. Do you think peers who have strict parents are less likely or more likely to take drugs? Permissive parents: more likely or less likely?

5. Do you think drug use in your school is increasing or decreasing?

Drinking and Driving

The action takes place at a junior high party
which is just beginning to break up.

Thelma: We'd better call your mother to pick us up. Kids are starting to leave.

Jean: OK. I'll be right back. (*She exits, then re-enters a few moments later.*)

Thelma: Is she on her way?

Jean: No, my Uncle Bob and Aunt Martha are still there, but she's calling Tim to have him pick us up.

Thelma: Your brother, Tim? I thought he was away at college.

Jean: He is. I mean he was. He's home just for the weekend.

Thelma: But why is your mother calling him if he's home?

Jean: He's over at his friend's house. They're watching videos. Mom said he can take us home and then go back to what he was doing. He's only a few blocks from here.

Scene ii

Tim *and* **Ernie** *are sitting side by side on two chairs which represent a car. As the lights come up, both jerk backward in the chairs as if* **Tim** *had slammed on the brakes.* **Thelma** *and* **Jean,** *along with several classmates, are standing nearby.*

Jason: Wow, he is really burning rubber!

Jean: Come on, Thelma. Tim's here.

Jean *runs to the car.* **Thelma** *hangs back.* **Jean** *pantomimes opening the passenger side door and sees* **Ernie.***)*

Jean: Oh, hi, Ernie. I didn't know you'd be with Tim.

Ernie: (*Holding a can of beer in his hand*) I just came along for the ride.

Tim: (*He has one hand on the imaginary wheel, and in the other one, he holds a can of beer*) Hurry, and get in, Sis, you're interrupting our evening.

Jean: (*Pantomimes opening the back door and starts to get in. Stops when she notices* **Thelma** *isn't with her*) Sorry about that, Tim. (*Looking at the place where she'd last seen* **Thelma**) Now, why is Thelma still standing there?

Jean *motions for* **Thelma** *to come.* **Thelma** *shakes her head.*

Jean: (*Exasperated*) What's the matter with her? Just a minute guys. I'll be right back.

Tim: Well, hurry up.

Jean: (*Running back to where* **Thelma** *stands*) Come on. They're in a hurry.

Thelma: Go on without me. I'll call my mom.

Jean: What's wrong with you? Your mom expects you to ride home with us.

Thelma: My mom also expects me to get home in one piece.

Jean: What are you talking about?

Thelma: Didn't you see the way Tim was driving when he sped up to the curb? I knew he was drinking even before I saw the beer can in his hand.

Jean: He'll drive safely with us in the car. He's not drunk.

Thelma: No, I really can't. I promised my parents I'd never get in the car with a person who was drinking and driving.

Jean: They'll never know. Now come on. Tim's going to get angry if he has to wait much longer.

Thelma: Thanks, Jean, but I'll just call my mom. She won't mind coming after me.

Jean: Whatever you say. Talk to you later. (*She pantomimes getting into the car.*)

Questions for Discussion

1. Jean applies peer pressure to get Thelma into the car. Do you think most kids could resist the kind of pressure that Thelma does? Could you?

2. Thelma says she had promised her mother that she would not get into a car with anyone who was drinking and driving. Do you think she really had made this promise, or does she use this excuse so Jean will not keep pressuring her? Have you ever said that your parent would not let you do something when you found it hard to say no?

3. Do you think Jean's mother knew that Tim would be drinking? If so, why do you think she sent him?

4. Discuss some of the accidents that you are aware of that were caused by drinking and driving.

Alcohol Included

The action takes place in a peer helping class.
*A guest speaker, **Mr. Bennett,***
has just talked to the class.

Mr. Bennett: That just about does it. I've given you a general overview of the most common drugs and their effects. Now I wonder if you have any questions.

*Bill's hand quickly shoots up, and **Mr. Bennett***
nods to him.

Bill: You listed alcohol as a drug commonly used by teenagers. I don't understand why you listed it under the category of drugs. Isn't it just something to give a person a little pick-up, maybe a little buzz?

Juan: That's what my dad uses it for. Every evening when he gets home from work, he collapses in his big chair in front of the television and asks Mom to bring him a beer. Says he needs it after working on the shipping dock all day.

Mr. Bennett: (*Looking at* **Juan**) A lot of adults drink a beer or a cocktail at the end of the day, but (*turning to* **Bill**) it's still a drug.

Bill: You're kidding.

Mr. Bennett: No, I'm very serious. And I want to make it clear to all of you that alcohol, like other drugs, has caused some people a lot of problems.

Tammy: You're referring to people who become alcoholics?

Mr. Bennett: Yes, I'm referring to the people who can't drink alcohol without becoming addicted to it.

Wanda: But it takes a long time to become an alco—I mean one of those people like my Uncle Clyde. He's old, in his forties.

Mr. Bennett: No, that isn't true. It doesn't take a long time. In fact, there are teenage alcoholics. You probably know some of them, but just don't know they're alcoholics. In fact, they may not know it themselves.

Tammy: I know someone like that. A high school friend of my brother. For a couple of years he didn't know he was. But when he finally realized it, he spent six weeks in a drug rehab center.

Bill: I know people can get addicted to alcohol—we see all that on TV—but I just didn't think it should be listed under the category of a drug.

Juan: Man, I think the same thing. When I think of drugs, I think of things like crack and acid. You know, the real thing.

Mr. Bennett: Alcohol is the real thing too. It can be just as dangerous as any of the other drugs.

Tammy: Like when someone gets behind the wheel of a car after drinking.

Mr. Bennett: That's true. But I was thinking of dangerous from the standpoint of what it can do to the human body.

Juan: Doesn't seem to hurt my dad. He's as strong as an ox, and he drinks several beers every night. On the weekend, even more.

Mr. Bennett: Sometimes we don't see the damage that's being done until it's very serious, like cirrhosis of the liver. Or it may be a health problem secondary to the drinking.

Wanda: What do you mean by that?

Mr. Bennett: An example might be a father who comes home at night, sits down in front of the television, and fills up on beer instead of eating a nourishing meal.

Bill: But it can't be dangerous to our bodies at this age, can it?

Wanda: Of course, it can. You can drink and drive, and get yourself killed. To me that's dangerous to the body.

Bill: I mean, other than that.

Mr. Bennett: One of the signs of an alcoholic is blacking out. That means that the body has been affected to the degree that one loses consciousness.

Bill: Can that happen at our age?

Mr. Bennett: Yes, I'm afraid so. Some alcoholics are a lot younger than you are. But I don't want you to get the wrong impression. A person can be an alcoholic without blacking out.

Juan: I don't think many of us take drinking very seriously because we see so many adults who do it.

Bill: That's right. We don't see that many adults taking drugs. That's why it's still hard for me to think of alcohol as a drug.

Mr. Bennett: That's exactly why we're concerned about the drinking among teenagers today. Other drugs may be on the decline, but alcohol consumption isn't. Just as Juan said, kids don't see drinking as any big deal.

Tammy: I see what you mean. We are better educated about other drugs, but since most of us don't classify alcohol as a drug, we don't worry about what effect it can have on us.

Mr. Bennett: I think that about sums it up, Tammy. Any more questions before the bell rings?

Questions for Discussion

1. The effect of alcohol on the body is brought up in the discussion. What are some of the effects?

2. Teenagers can become alcoholics in a shorter period of time than adults. Is this statement true or false?

3. Do you think Mr. Bennett uses scare tactics when answering the questions? What do you think of scare tactics?

4. Juan does not seem to think that his dad drinking several beers every night and on weekends is any big deal. Can someone be an alcoholic when the only alcohol they drink is beer?

5. Tammy seems to know more about alcohol than the others in her class. Why do you think this might be?

EATING DISORDERS

Mother Is Too Thin

The action takes place in Sibyl's room at home.
*She and **Katie** and **Evelyn** are playing records*
and talking.

Sibyl: So what did you think of the guest speaker today?

Katie: Pretty gross.

Sibyl: I can't understand that kind of thing. Why would anyone want to starve themselves? And what about those pictures where the people were all skin and bones. They looked terrible.

Katie: I know. Like they were all dying from starvation and still thought they were too fat.

Sibyl: Or the people who ate all that food and then threw up. That's what really grossed me out. Besides the fact that they ruined their teeth and did all those other terrible things to their bodies...

Katie: You're awfully quiet, Evelyn.

134

Evelyn: I guess so.

Sibyl: Is something the matter?

Evelyn: I don't know.

Sibyl: It sure sounds like it. Are you having a problem?

Evelyn: Maybe.

Sibyl: We're friends, right? So if you want to talk about it...

Evelyn: I'm worried about my mom, that's all.

Katie: What do you mean? Is she sick or something?

Evelyn: It's like...like those people the speaker in assembly talked about. My mom's just like that. She keeps losing weight and losing weight. She never eats anything except green salad with vinegar. Not even real dressing. And all she ever drinks is a glass of water. Sometimes that's all she has for a whole meal. She says that's all she needs.

Sibyl: Oh, wow, are you sure? Maybe it's just when you're at home. Maybe she eats a big lunch.

Evelyn: I wish that were it, but she keeps talking about wanting to lose five more pounds. Then when she does, she still thinks she's too fat. I mean sometimes she doesn't eat anything all day long. She says she's not hungry.

Katie: Have you talked to her about it?

Evelyn: Not really. I've just told her she's getting awfully thin.

Katie: What does she say?

Evelyn: That I'm just trying to be nice; that she's really fat. She can tell when she looks in the mirror. (*Starts to cry*) I don't know what to do. I'm worried. I mean since my dad left...

Sibyl: You think your mother's anorexic?

Evelyn: I'm sure she is. I mean, I didn't have a name for it before today. I didn't know anything about it, except that I knew something was wrong.

Katie: That's pretty serious. What do you think you can do? Is there anyone you can talk to?

Evelyn: Not really. Not since my dad left. I mean I hardly even talk to him anymore. He's got his new family now.

Katie: What about your grandparents?

Evelyn: They're too far away. What could they do anyway?

Sibyl: Could you talk to someone at school? Maybe a peer helper or someone. At least they might be able to tell you how to get help.

Evelyn: It has to be my mother's decision, doesn't it? I mean she's the one who has to find help.

Sibyl: I'm sorry, Evelyn. I really am.

Katie: Me too.

Evelyn: I know. I'm so worried. I wish I could wave a magic wand and make everything OK.

Questions for Discussion

1. Have you known anyone with an eating disorder such as the ones described by Sibyl, Katie, and Evelyn?

2. Sibyl says that hearing about people who eat and throw up their food really "grosses her out." Is she describing a person who has anorexia or bulimia?

3. One of the symptoms of bulimia Sibyl talks about is damaged teeth. What are some other symptoms?

4. Do you think Evelyn's mother is in physical danger? Can someone die from anorexia?

5. Starving oneself and continuing to think one is fat are symptoms of anorexia. Can you name other symptoms?

6. Evelyn said that it had to be her mother's decision to get help. Do you agree with her? Why or why not?

Embarrassed to Dress in Gym

*The action takes place in the counseling office
at school.*

Mr. Sanders: So what did you want to see me about, Eric?

Eric: Everyone makes fun of me, you know?

Mr. Sanders: I'm not sure I do.

Eric: Just look at me. Don't you understand?

Mr. Sanders: Tell me, Eric.

Eric: I'm fat. They call me a tub of guts and maybe they're right. 'Cause that's what I am.

Mr. Sanders: Sounds like you're pretty down on yourself.

Eric: I'm embarrassed even to show up at school. And do you want to know the worst part?

Mr. Sanders: What's that?

Eric: When I had to get undressed in gym.

Mr. Sanders: (*Looking at Eric's records*) I see by your records that you aren't taking gym anymore, are you?

Eric: No, I'm not. But the other kids remember. You can't
believe all the terrible things they said. I mean it was
the first week of school, and everyone had to get undressed and get into shorts and a T-shirt. I felt so bad
my stomach hurt. It made me sick.

Mr. Sanders: I can tell it must have been very difficult.

Eric: I've never been so embarrassed. Even worse than
that, I never wanted to show my face again.

Mr. Sanders: Is that why you aren't taking gym?

Eric: Yeah. Mom got me a doctor's excuse to skip it. I
couldn't go through it again. Particularly when we had
to take showers. Everyone pointed and laughed and
said all kinds of things.

Mr. Sanders: And that's really bothered you, hasn't it?

Eric: Wouldn't it bother you?

Mr. Sanders: No one likes to be made fun of.

Eric: And I just can't have kids making fun of me all the
time. I wish...I wish I just didn't have to be here at all.

Mr. Sanders: You felt completely humiliated, and you
can't forget it.

Eric: It's not as bad now as it was in gym. But the other
kids still laugh. They think it's funny. I wish I lived on
a desert island or something and never had to face
anyone else again.

Mr. Sanders: Have you ever tried to do anything about your weight?

Eric: You mean like trying to reduce?

Mr. Sanders: Or changing your diet.

Eric: I tried all kinds of things, but I just can't help myself. I don't want to eat all that food, but when I get home, I head right to the refrigerator. And then I'm ashamed of myself and that makes it worse.

Mr. Sanders: Have you talked to anyone else about this? Have you told them the things you're telling me?

Eric: Mom took me to a doctor. He said that I might outgrow it.

Mr. Sanders: Do you think he was right?

Eric: No. It was only because my mom kept saying it. And he finally agreed that maybe she was right. But he knew that wasn't true. I mean he gave me a diet. A really strict one.

Mr. Sanders: How did that work out?

Eric: For awhile, it was OK. Mom fixed the right things, and I tried to eat just what she fixed. But then I started to sneak other food—things from the refrigerator or candy and cupcakes—stuff like that—I bought with my allowance. Finally, my mom just gave up.

Mr. Sanders: How did you feel about that? About her giving up.

Eric: Not very good. But it was my fault.

Mr. Sanders: It seems to me that part of the problem is your feelings of low self-esteem. Do you think that's possible?

Eric: Yeah, I know. I'm always ashamed and embarrassed. And I feel I'm not worth very much if I can't do what I'm supposed to. Mr. Sanders, I don't want be fat, but I can't stop eating. Even when I don't want to eat, it's like I have to. And then when kids call me names—like in gym—I feel all empty inside. And the only way to feel better is to eat.

Questions for Discussion

1. Eric talks about how he felt when the kids teased him about his weight. What are some of the words he uses to describe his feelings?

2. Have you ever had a weight problem? Describe how you felt when someone made fun of you. Do you ever comment on someone's weight in a joking way, thinking that person doesn't mind?

3. Eric said that he stayed on his diet for a while but then began to sneak food from the refrigerator. Can you identify with this? Talk about some of the problems you have had with dieting.

4. What have you found to be the most effective when you've tried to change your weight? Did you get support from another person?

5. Mr. Sanders says that he thought part of Eric's problem was low self-esteem. Do you agree or disagree? Why?

FRIENDSHIP

Best Friend

The action takes place at Peter's home.

Peter: Did you come over here to tell me *that!?* I don't believe you. Don't you know a guy doesn't do that to his best friend?

Zack: I'm not doing anything to you.

Peter: Right!

Zack: It's not like you and Amy are going steady. In fact, you're not even dating.

Peter: Not yet. But I told you at the beginning of the year that Amy was the girl that I intended to invite to the graduation dance.

Zack: Well, it is only two weeks away, and you haven't asked her yet.

Peter: I'm still thinking about the right way to do it.

Zack: By the time you get up your courage, she'll already be going with someone else.

Peter: Sure she will. (*Pause*) You! My best friend that I thought I could trust.

Zack: Look, Peter, I haven't asked her yet. I wanted to come over here tonight and tell you what I planned to do. Now if I wasn't your friend, do you think I'd bother?

Peter: (*Exasperated*) But you don't seem to understand. Best friends don't do that to one another. They don't butt in.

Zack: I think I'd better just be honest with you, Peter. Gloria told me today that Amy wanted me to ask her.

Peter: What! Why would Gloria say that to you?

Zack: Because she and Amy are best friends, and apparently they talk to one another about things like that.

Peter: You're just making this up, so you won't feel guilty about asking her.

Zack: I'm telling you the truth. She wants to go to the dance with me. Now if I don't ask her, someone else will and neither one of them will have a good time because she wants to go with me.

Peter: You're saying that if I ask her tomorrow before you do, she won't have a good time with me because it will really be you that she'd rather be with?

Zack: I'm only telling you what Gloria told me. But they *are* best friends.

Peter: (*Dejectedly*) I guess so. (*Pause*) Go ahead and ask her. I'll just go alone. (*Under his breath*) Fine best friend you are!

Scene ii

The action takes place at Gloria's house.

Gloria: I thought you'd be happy. I really went out of my way to do this for you.

Amy: Thanks, but I'd rather you'd not put yourself out.

Gloria: That's what friends are for. To look out for one another.

Amy: You thought I needed looking out for?

Gloria: Well, let's face it. It's only two weeks until the dance, and you don't know who you're going with yet.

Amy: Or even if I'm going.

Gloria: Don't talk like that. Of course, you're going. It's in the bag. Zack will ask you tomorrow.

Amy: He said that?

Gloria: Well, not exactly. But I know he wants to. I just helped him along a little by telling him that I knew you'd like to go with him.

Amy: You did what?!

Gloria: Oh, don't get so excited. If you just knew a little more about boys, you'd know these things.

Amy: What things?

Gloria: A boy likes to know that a girl likes him before he asks her. That way he knows he won't get turned down. Boys don't like to be rejected. It's not in keeping with their macho image.

Amy: What you don't understand, Gloria, is that I don't like Zack, and I really don't want to go to the dance with him.

Gloria: At least you'll have a date. We can get dressed over here at my house before the dance. Then afterward you can come back over and spend the night. We can talk about what everyone wore and who they were with. It'll be a lot of fun.

Amy: It sounds good, but—

Gloria: But what?

Amy: I just wanted to go with someone else.

Gloria: Who, for heaven's sake?

Amy: (*Pauses*) This may sound real strange to you, but I've kind of thought that Peter might ask me. He's been so nice to me all year.

Gloria: Peter?

Amy: I know he's never asked me on a date before, but I thought he might get his courage up for this last dance of the year. He's quiet, but I really enjoy being around him.

Gloria: You sound like you really like the guy.

Amy: I guess I do. But maybe it was just wishful thinking to imagine that he would actually ask me. He's probably already asked someone else.

Gloria: Probably so. Now will you go with Zack when he asks you?

Amy: (*Dejectedly*) I guess so.

Gloria: Can't you act a little bit more excited about what your best friend has done for you? A thank you might be nice.

Amy: Thanks, Gloria. You really are a good friend.

Questions for Discussion

1. Do you think Zack should ask Amy for a date, knowing that Peter wants to? If Zack was not Peter's best friend, would your answer have been different?

2. How do you feel about Zack's going to Peter's house and telling him about his intentions?

3. Is Gloria being a best friend by trying to get Amy a date? Why or why not?

4. Should Amy be angry at Gloria for being untruthful about her to Zack?

5. Who do you think will enjoy the dance the most: Amy, Peter, Zack, or Gloria? Who will enjoy it the least?

6. If you were Peter's best friend, what would you have done differently? What would you have done differently if you were Amy's best friend?

My Friend and I Argue

*The action begins as **Brenda** and **Liz** are
walking to school together.*

Brenda: But you said you wanted to see the movie.

Liz: No, I didn't. I said I might want to.

Brenda: Well, I've already talked my mother into driving us to the mall—no easy feat since she had to rearrange her own plans.

Liz: You just shouldn't have done that before we agreed on what we wanted to do.

Brenda: I thought we had agreed.

Liz: No. Only *you* had agreed, and you went right ahead thinking I'd do what you wanted. That's the way it always is with you, and I'm getting a little tired of it;

Brenda: You have a very poor memory. Last week we went bowling because you thought Jack and Frank might be there.

Liz: You're still ticked off about Frank being there with Hillary. That wasn't my fault!

Brenda: (*Raising her voice*) I didn't say it was. I said that we did what you wanted to do, and you were the one who came up with that dumb idea.

Liz: (*Loudly*) It wouldn't have been a dumb idea if Frank had been there alone and had noticed you.

> **Steve, Henry,** and **Melanie** *approach, walking from behind them.*

Steve: You two arguing again? I don't know why you enjoy being friends when you argue all the time.

Liz: We weren't arguing! And what are you doing coming up behind us and eavesdropping?

Henry: No one needs to eavesdrop. We could hear you clear down to the end of the block.

Melanie: Well, maybe not that far, Hank.

Steve: I could hear well enough to know you were arguing about Frank. Must be nice for him to have both of you fighting over him.

Liz: You'd better not start a rumor like that. I wouldn't be caught dead with Frank.

> **Brenda** *gives her a quizzical look.*

Henry: Well, what's the problem? Something's not right between you two.

Brenda: We were just having a slight disagreement.

Steve: Sounded like an all-out war to me. I can't understand why girls argue all the time. You don't find us guys doing it.

Melanie: Maybe that's because guys don't communicate with each other as well as girls do.

Henry: You mean arguing is good communication?

Steve: If so, I'd just as soon not communicate so well.

Liz: What you don't seem to understand is that girls can argue and still remain friends. That's what good friendship is.

Brenda: You guys get mad at one another, get into a fist fight, and never talk again. What a waste!

Steve: I know some girls who get into pretty good fights themselves. Lots of hairpulling.

Liz: Not that many girls fight like that. I know I don't.

Henry: Maybe not, but you argue like you're about ready to start hitting anytime.

Brenda: (*Looking at* **Liz**) We aren't even still unhappy with one another, are we?

Liz: I guess that depends. Do you still insist on seeing that movie tonight?

Questions for Discussion

1. Is arguing necessary? Is there a better way to communicate? Discuss some ways.

2. What can you do to stop an argument after it has started?

3. What could Liz have done differently once she found out that Brenda had already made plans for the two of them?

4. Steve says that guys do not argue as much as girls do. Do you think he is right? Why or why not?

5. If one of your friendships is destroyed because of an argument or a fight, what can you do to establish it again?

Why Don't I Have More Friends?

As the scene opens, **Ellen** *and* **Sue** *are sitting on the grass in front of school, waiting for rides home.*

Sue: You're going to Beth's party Saturday night, aren't you?

Ellen: I don't know.

Sue: Come on, Ellen, you know you're going. You don't have to deny it to make me feel better.

Ellen: I feel bad that you weren't invited. I just don't understand why you weren't.

Sue: I understand. I'm never invited to any party except the ones you have. The other kids just don't seem to want me around. I wonder why you do.

Ellen: I want you around because you're my friend. The other kids just haven't gotten to know you. I'm sure they'll act differently when they do.

Sue: I'm not exactly the new kid on the block any longer. I've been here for five months. That's plenty of time for them to get to know me if they wanted to. (*Pause*) Do you think I'll ever have any friends at this school other than you?

Ellen: Of course you will.

Sue: Then why is it taking so long?

Ellen: You have to remember that this town has only one middle school and most of these kids have the same friends they made in elementary school.

Sue: In other words, they all keep their same friends when they enter middle school, and they see no need to expand their group.

Ellen: It's something like that, I guess.

Sue: Sounds like cliques to me.

Ellen: Maybe. But they really don't intend to be mean. I think they just don't know how it feels to be left out.

Sue: And you do?

Ellen: I moved to this town three years ago when I was still in elementary school. I felt the same way then that you do now. I didn't think I'd ever be invited to anything. And I wasn't for the longest time.

Sue: But you finally were. What made it happen?

Ellen: I did.

Sue: You did?

Ellen: Yes, I did. I worked at it. I was determined that I'd make friends with the others, and I kept trying till it happened.

Sue: I'd never do that. If they don't want to be friends with me, then I don't want to be friends with them.

Ellen: You don't mean that.

Sue: Of course, I do. I'm just as good as they are, but if they want to be snobbish and not include me, then that's OK with me.

Ellen: There's your mom driving up. We'll talk again on Monday.

Sue: Fine. (*Calling back over her shoulder as she walks to the car*) Have a good time at the party tomorrow night.

Questions for Discussion

1. How does one make friends? Give examples.

2. Do you think Sue will ever have a lot of friends at her new school? Why or why not?

3. Why do you think Ellen befriended Sue? What else could Ellen do to help Sue gain more friends?

4. Sue says that if the other kids don't want to be friends with her then she doesn't want to be friends with them. Do you think she means it? Why or why not?

GANGS

Gangs Killed My Brother

The action occurs in front of the school before the start of classes. **Tracy** *and* **Jan** *are standing by the steps and talking when* **Sylvia** *arrives.*

Tracy: Hi, Sylvia. I haven't seen you for a few days. Have you been ill?

Sylvia: No.

Tracy: Is something wrong?

Sylvia: My brother's dead. He was killed.

Jan: Oh, no! What happened?

Sylvia: A drive-by shooting. He was out playing on the sidewalk... (*She starts to cry.*)

Tracy: Oh, Sylvia, I'm sorry. That's awful.

Sylvia: He was five years old. Just a little kid. My dad always said he wanted to leave the neighborhood. But we couldn't afford it. And now this happened.

Tracy: Five! I thought you had an older brother.

Sylvia: I do. He's fifteen.

Jan: Did they find out who did this? The police, I mean?

Sylvia: Oh, sure! The police don't care.

Tracy: What do you mean?

Sylvia: You know what it's like in my neighborhood. The police stay away from there.

Tracy: I don't think that's true. My cousin's on the force. That's the area he patrols.

Sylvia: What does it matter anyhow?

Jan: What do you mean?

Sylvia: It's the gangs. Nothing's going to stop them. They were after my brother. My older brother, I mean. And they shot Joey instead.

Tracy: They didn't kill him deliberately, did they?

Sylvia: Joey? Of course they did. Anything to stir things up. (*She wipes away her tears*) They wanted to get back at my brother's gang, maybe even at my brother himself. Bobby, I mean, not Joey. I'm so worried.

Jan: What do you mean?

Sylvia: You don't know anything, do you? (*She shakes her head*) I'm sorry. But I'm afraid for Bobby now. I mean, his gang's going to try to even the score, and he's going to be killed too.

Tracy: Maybe not. Maybe things will be OK.

Sylvia: Look, Tracy, I know you're only trying to help, but you don't know anything about it. It's a thing of honor, you know what I mean? When one gang does something, the other one has to get back at them, no matter what. No matter how many kids are hurt or killed.

Tracy: Isn't there anything that can be done?

Sylvia: What? Gangs are a fact of life. All the boys have to belong. They don't have a choice—except to move away or...or get killed like Joey did. I wish...I wish we could just move or something.

Jan: But you said you can't?

Sylvia: My father's out of work half the time. Mom tries to help out, but she can barely read and write. There's just no hope. It's just the way things are.

Tracy: There must be someone who can help.

Sylvia: A fairy godmother! I don't think so. Nobody cares.

Tracy: That's not true, Sylvia. I care a lot.

Sylvia: But what good does that do? Joey's dead, and we're still there. And soon Bobby will be dead. That's the way things are.

Jan: Not everyone gets killed.

Sylvia: But a lot of them do. Like I said, that's just the way it is.

Jan: I wish...

Sylvia: You wish you could change it? Well, yeah, so do I.

Questions for Discussion

1. Sylvia says to Jan, "You don't know anything, do you?" Discuss what you know about gangs, either firsthand or what you've read.

2. Do you think the gang killed Joey intentionally, or was it just a random drive by shooting?

3. Sylvia feels that no ones cares. How would you have shown her that you cared?

4. What do you think is the most effective way to deal with gangs?

5. Do you think that Sylvia's father was right in wanting to move away? What can a parent do when he or she can't afford to move away?

What Color Are You Wearing?

The action takes place out on the street.
Roberto, *a boy new to the area, is walking home*
from school. **Winston** *and* **Mitchell** *are*
standing on the corner, watching him approach.

Winston: Hey, kid, what are you doing here?

Roberto: (*Startled*) What?

Mitchell: What he means is, why are you wearing those colors?

Roberto: What colors?

Winston: Look, man, are you stupid or something?

Roberto: (*Becoming angry*) I don't know what you're talking about.

Mitchell: What we're talking about, man, is why someone wearing the colors of another gang is dumb enough to come into this neighborhood.

Roberto: These are just my clothes. I don't belong to any gang.

Winston: I think you came here to cause trouble. That's what I think.

Roberto: Look, I just moved here. I don't know anything about any gangs.

Mitchell: Well, I think you're lying.

Roberto: I'm not lying. I just moved here a couple of days ago. I used to live in another part of the country. I don't know about any gangs.

Winston: What do you say, Mitchell? Don't you think we should show him what it's like to come into this neighborhood wearing colors like that?

Mitchell: I think you're right, Winston. We'll teach him a lesson.

They start to advance on **Roberto,** *who tries to back away.*

Roberto: I'm telling you guys I just moved here. I don't even know what you're talking about.

Mitchell: Yeah, right.

Winston: You know, I haven't seen him around. Where did you say you live, man?

Roberto: A couple of blocks down the street. We just moved in last Friday.

Mitchell: Well, maybe.

Winston: How about if we tag along? And if you're lying, you're in deep trouble. Understand?

Roberto: OK, all right.

Mitchell: But a bit of advice. Don't go wearing those colors again. Understand? Not in this neighborhood. Unless you don't value your life.

Roberto: I didn't know—

Winston: Well, now you do, all right, man?

Questions for Discussion

1. Talk about some gangs that you are aware of. Are they known by their colors? Do you know what they are?

2. Do you think Roberto will be able to live in his new neighborhood and not join the gang? Why or why not?

3. Winston and Mitchell appear to be pretty tough in their demands. Do you think they will protect their territory as they say they will?

4. Talk about how gangs feel about their territorial rights.

GOALS

Is It Worth It?

Action takes place as the bell rings at the end of the school day. **Stacy** *and* **Jennifer** *start talking as they walk toward the door.*

Stacy: What if she isn't right?

Jennifer: Right about what?

Stacy: What if she isn't right when she says that it will all be worth it?

Jennifer: You mean my mom?

Stacy: Yes, what if is she isn't right when she says your spending every afternoon at the ice rink is worth it?

Jennifer: Mom says that everyone who has a goal and reaches it has to make sacrifices to get there.

Stacy: Sure she does.

Jennifer: What do you mean by that?

Stacy: It's you who's making all the sacrifices. Never having any time to spend with your friends.

Jennifer: That's not fair. Mom makes sacrifices too.

Stacy: Like what?

Jennifer: She has to pick me up every afternoon after school and take me to Skateland.

Stacy: Big deal.

Jennifer: Then she has to wait for me for two hours—three on days that I take lessons.

Stacy: What else does she have to do?

Jennifer: She has to take me to exhibitions and contests on the weekends. She doesn't even get to be at home with Dad and Joey very often.

Stacy: (*Frustrated*) No! I don't mean what else does she do. I mean what else does she *have* to do? She doesn't have a job like my mother. Joey's in high school and you're already eleven. What does she have to do with her time other than push you?

Jennifer: (*Becoming agitated*) That's not fair to my mom, Stacy. (*Emphatically*) I want to practice. I like to skate.

Stacy: I'm sorry, Jennifer. I guess I was coming on a little too strong. I just remember how it used to be—when we had fun after school—before you started skating.

Jennifer: I remember those times too. And I miss them just like you do. But Mom and I have this goal that I'll get to the Olympics some day.

Stacy: I know. Every since the two of you watched the Olympics together last year.

Jennifer: Each day since, we talk about getting there. We've even designed the costume I'll wear—just in our heads, of course.

Stacy: But that will take years and years of practice.

Jennifer: I know. (*Looks out the door*) There's Mom. 'Bye, Stacy.

Questions for Discussion

1. Are goals usually worth the effort it takes to reach them?

2. What are some of your goals?

3. Name some of the celebrities you know who sacrificed to get where they are today.

4. Why do you think Jennifer's skating makes Stacy unhappy?

5. Is Jennifer's dream hers or her mother's? Or both? Why?

HOME LIFE

I Shouldn't Have to Do Chores

*The action takes place in Brenda's room before
her mother and father get home from work.
It's late afternoon; school has been out for about
an hour.*

Heather: Do you think you better get started with your chores before your mom gets home? I said I'd help you.

Brenda: I'm just not going to do them, that's all.

Heather: Won't you get in trouble?

Brenda: So what? I don't care.

Heather: Come on, Brenda. What do you have to do? Vacuum and dust the living room and what else?

Brenda: Clean my bedroom.

Heather: (*Looking around and kidding* **Brenda**) You and what army?

Brenda: (*Picks up a pillow and throws it at* **Heather**) Think it's bad, do you?

Heather: What would you like me to do?

Brenda: I said I wasn't going to do it.

Heather: I don't understand.

Brenda: Why should I? I go to school all day, and then I have homework.

Heather: Who's going to do it if you don't?

Brenda: My mom, of course.

Heather: But she works.

Brenda: Yeah, and she doesn't have to. It was a lot nicer when she didn't. Back then she did all this stuff she's trying to shove off onto me.

Heather: I have to clean my room and do chores, and my mom doesn't even work. She never has.

Brenda: Well, that's you, and this is me.

Heather: Thanks a lot.

Brenda: Sorry, I didn't mean anything.

Heather: Do you seriously think you shouldn't have to do anything around the house? That your mom should have to do everything?

Brenda: Yeah, I do.

Heather: I've always had to help out. As long as I can remember. And sure, sometimes I'd rather be doing other things too. But if I'm really in a bind, Mom understands.

Brenda: Well, maybe you're used to it, but I'm not. And like I said, my mom doesn't have to work. We always got along on the money Dad made.

Heather: Why's she working then?

Brenda: (*Mimicking her mother's voice*) Self-fulfillment. Whatever that means. She just doesn't like to do housework.

Heather: (*Teasing*) I wonder who else doesn't like it, huh?

Brenda: Well, I don't.

Heather: You told me you wanted to be a veterinarian, isn't that right?

Brenda: Yeah, so what?

Heather: What if someday you have kids, and you're working? Are you going to want to come home and do all the work? Don't you think your kids should help out?

Brenda: How should I know?

Heather: You want to be a veterinarian, and your mother wants to do what she's doing. Is that so bad?

Brenda: The situation's entirely different.

Heather: How?

Brenda: Mom works in a clothing store. That's not like being a vet.

Heather: Oh, so what you want to do is better, huh?

Brenda: I don't want to argue, Heather.

Heather: Come on then, let's get started. You get things out of the way, and I'll start to vacuum.

Brenda: You don't have to do that.

Heather: I know I don't, but you're my friend.

Brenda: I still think my mother should do it. After all, I have to go to school, but she doesn't have to work.

Heather: OK, Brenda, whatever you say.

Questions for Discussion

1. Heather asks Brenda, "Do you seriously think you shouldn't have to do anything around the house? That your mom should have to do everything?" Do you agree or disagree with Brenda's answer? Why?

2. Heather has a different attitude about doing household chores than Brenda does. Which girl's position do you think represents most teenagers?

3. Do you think Brenda's mother should work outside the home when she doesn't have to? Should mothers who stay at home have to do all the chores themselves?

4. Do you think Brenda and her mother could work out their problem if they talked about it? What should be Brenda's approach? What should her mother say to Brenda?

Father Plays Favorites

The action occurs in the school cafeteria at lunchtime. **Jesse, Tiffany** *and* **Janette** *are sharing a table.*

Jesse: I hate my stepfather. I thought I was going to like him, but I don't.

Tiffany: What's he like?

Jesse: I don't know. I shouldn't even be talking about it. I mean they're his kids—Michelle and Cynthia. It's just... See, he does all these things for them—

Janette: And doesn't do the same things for you.

Jesse: That's right.

Tiffany: Don't you think that's natural? They're his kids. He knows them a lot better.

Jesse: It's not fair; we're supposed to be a family.

Janette: Do you get along with his two kids?

174

Jesse: Michelle and Cynthia? Sure. They're both a lot younger than I am. But I like them OK.

Tiffany: Maybe that's it then. He has to do a lot more for them 'cause they can't do it for themselves. They're too young.

Jesse: That isn't what I mean.

Janette: What do you mean?

Jesse: He takes them places and buys them things. Just him and them. He never asks me to come along.

Janette: What about your mom? Does she buy things for you?

Jesse: Of course she does.

Tiffany: I think what Janette means is that maybe your mom does more for you, and your stepfather does more for his kids.

Jesse: I don't think so. I mean when he takes Cynthia and Michelle shopping, Mom usually goes along and helps them pick things out.

Tiffany: Maybe it's because he feels he should take them.

Jesse: Then why doesn't he take me?

Tiffany: Maybe he feels that it's his duty. Maybe he doesn't even like it. A lot of men don't like to go shopping. My father doesn't.

Jesse: Yeah, but like when they have things at school—the open house, for instance. He went and so did Mom. But when I played the piano that time in assembly, he didn't come.

Janette: Maybe he had to work.

Jesse: Whose side are you on anyhow?

Janette: Your side, Jess, if there are any sides.

Tiffany: Do his two kids get a lot more things than you do? Clothes and stuff?

Jesse: No, not really. But Mom buys my stuff.

Tiffany: Well, that's what I meant. Maybe he feels he has to get things for his kids, rather than shoving the responsibility onto your mother. Maybe they think your mother should buy things for them.

Jesse: I don't know. I thought we were supposed to be a family.

Janette: It must be hard, I know. My cousin's mom left and her dad remarried. She hates her stepmom and feels she cares only about her own little boy.

Jesse: Yeah, but that doesn't help me feel better.

Tiffany: Have you talked to your mom about this?

Janette: Or even your stepfather?

Jesse: They'd only get mad.

Janette: How do you know that?

Jesse: I just do.

Tiffany: I'm not saying it's fair. Maybe it isn't. But maybe you should try to do something about it. I mean, what's your stepfather like?

Jesse: He treats me OK. Around the house, I mean. He doesn't try to boss me around or anything. He's a pretty neat guy, except...

Janette: Except that you still feel he loves his own kids a lot more than he loves you.

Jesse: I guess so. I said I hate him, but I really don't. Actually, I like him. I'm glad he and Mom got married. Except...I'd like him to take me places too.

Questions for Discussion

1. Why do you think Jesse's step-father does not do things for him as he does for his own children?

2. Have you had similar experiences with a step-father or step-mother? If so, how did you work it out, if you have?

3. Jesse thinks his step-father and his mother would get mad if he tried to talk to them. Do you think they would? How would you approach them if you were Jesse?

4. Jesse says, "I thought we were supposed to be a family." What do you think he means? Discuss what being a family means to you.

HOMOSEXUALITY

Mother's Friend

The action takes place in a peer helping class.

Rodney: Well, I think homosexuals can change the way they are, but they just don't want to.

Rhondelle: My mom was talking about that, and she said she thinks that they can't help the way they are. She said there was some doctor in San Diego who even proved that the brains of straight people and gay people are different.

Rodney: Yes, but I think it's wrong. At my church the preacher's always talking about how homosexuals go out and recruit young kids to their lifestyle. He says we all have to be careful.

Jodie: I have an uncle who never got married, and he's lived with the same man since before I was born.

Faith: What about lesbians?

Rodney: What about them?

Faith: Well, what I mean is, I don't think they're a whole lot different than we are. Just 'cause they love other women.

Rodney: I'm not sure people like that can love anyone at all.

Faith: Would you like to explain why you think that way?

Rodney: Well, how can a man love another man or a woman love another woman? My dad says that queers are an abomination in the eyes of the Lord. That's what the Bible says.

Faith: I asked my mom about that. It's because of these two women who live next door. And my mother says that the Bible really doesn't say anything about homosexuality being wrong.

Rhondelle: You've been awfully quiet, Lilly. Is there anything you'd like to say about all this?

Lilly: (*Sounding sullen*) No, I don't want to say anything.

Faith: It's sounds like something's bothering you. If you want to talk about it, we'd be glad to listen.

Rodney: Sure, Lilly. I didn't mean to hog all the time.

Lilly: Well, it's just that... Let's forget it.

Rhondelle: Are you sure?

Lilly: No, I'm not sure. I've never talked about this before. Not to anyone, and it's really hard.

Faith: If you want to go on, we'll be glad to listen.

Lilly: (*Taking a deep breath*) OK, it's about my mom.

Rhondelle: We're listening.

Lilly: You know I've never invited anyone home. (*She looks at* **Rhondelle**) Especially you, Rhondelle. And we're supposed to be best friends. And I suppose you've wondered about that, haven't you?

Rhondelle: There must be a reason.

Lilly: Yes, there is. You see I don't have a dad. In fact, I never did. I have a biological father, but I was conceived through artificial insemination. My mom never knew my father.

Faith: Would you like to explain that?

Lilly: Rodney, I'm especially worried that you won't understand.

Rodney: I'll try my best, you know that.

Lilly: OK. My mom lives with her friend. A special friend, another woman. So...so that's why I never invite anyone home.

Faith: It sounds like that bothers you.

Lilly: It bothers me. I didn't think anyone would understand. I mean it's not that I don't like Barbara. I do. I like her a lot. She's like... Well, she's like a second mother to me.

Rodney: You said you never had a father, Lilly.

Lilly: That's right. It's always been Mom and Barbara.

Faith: You introduced me to your mother at the open house. And there was someone else with her.

Lilly: That was Barbara. And now I'm all mixed up about it.

Faith: Would you like to explain what you mean?

Lilly: I'm ashamed about what people will think. What my classmates will think.

Rhondelle: It's not like you did anything wrong, Lilly. But I seem to hear you suggesting that you think it's wrong for your mom and Barbara to be together.

Lilly: I didn't say that!

Rhondelle: No, you didn't. I'm sorry.

Lilly: It's just that I'm ashamed to tell anyone about them. And then I'm ashamed of being ashamed. I mean I love my mom. And Barbara too. I love them both a lot. Maybe I even love Barbara as much as I love my mom.

Rhondelle: Most kids love their moms.

Lilly: I know, but I'm all mixed up. I don't know how I should feel.

Questions for Discussion

1. If you found out there was a homosexual in your class, would you treat that peer in the same way that you treat your other friends? Why or why not?

2. Do you think Lilly has reason to be concerned about telling her classmates about her mother's friend?

3. Lilly says, "I know, but I'm all mixed up. I don't know how I should feel." Who would you suggest that Lilly talk to in order to help her clarify her feelings?

4. This conversation takes place in a peer helping class where everything is confidential. Do you think Lilly would have shared her secret in another class, such as social studies or math?

Is Being Gay Inherited?

*The action takes place in the office of **Rev. Kurtz**, the youth minister at Jack's church. In order not to set up any barriers, **Rev. Kurtz** has moved into a straight-back chair placed at an angle to Jack's chair.*

Rev. Kurtz: How can I help you, Jack?

Jack: I'm worried.

Rev. Kurtz: Can you tell me why?

Jack: You know about my brother, right?

Rev. Kurtz: Patrick, you mean?

Jack: Yes.

Rev. Kurtz: What about him, Jack?

Jack: Well, you know he's...he's...

Rev. Kurtz: You mean that he's gay? He's a homosexual? Is that what you want to talk about?

Jack: You know my parents disowned him. They won't let me see him or talk to him on the phone. It's like he's dead or like he never existed.

Rev. Kurtz: I know that, Jack, and I'm sorry. I suppose that's something your parents felt they had to do.

Jack: It isn't fair. He can't help what he's like. Can he?

Rev. Kurtz: That's what some people think. There are others who say homosexuals can change.

Jack: What do you think?

Rev. Kurtz: Is that important?

Jack: What if it's inherited? What if Jack couldn't help it? What if he wanted to change but couldn't?

Rev. Kurtz: Why? Have you talked to him about this?

Jack: (*Shaking his head*) No.

Rev. Kurtz: Then I'm not sure I see what this is all about.

Jack: Well, if it's inherited, and I think maybe it is, that means...

Rev. Kurtz: I think I see. You're worried that you might be—

Jack: Yes. I'm afraid I might turn out to be gay.

Rev. Kurtz: And you think that would be a bad thing?

Jack: Well, my parents...

Rev. Kurtz: Disowned Patrick. Right?

Jack: Yes.

Rev. Kurtz: And you think they might disown you.

Jack: What if I have those feelings? What if I'm already gay?

Rev. Kurtz: Jack, I think you're a little young to take on that burden. If I were you, I wouldn't worry about it. Not yet.

Jack: What do you mean?

Rev. Kurtz: How can you know what you'll be like when you're older?

Jack: What if I already...like other guys?

Rev. Kurtz: Feel attracted to them, you mean.

Jack: What if I do?

Rev. Kurtz: Psychologists tell us that people go through a stage of being attracted to members of their own sex. It's a natural thing.

Jack: Then you don't think I'm going to be gay? You don't think it's inherited?

Rev. Kurtz: There's a lot of disagreement about that, Jack. Some people feel it is a physical thing—whether inherited or not. Others feel it's a choice, even a learned behavior.

Jack: I don't think Patrick could help it.

Rev. Kurtz: I'm sorry, but I can't give you pat answers. It's impossible. But there's one thing I do know.

Jack: What is it?

Rev. Kurtz: If I were you, I wouldn't worry about something like this for a few more years. I really doubt you can know yet how things will develop.

Jack: (*He stands.*) Thanks, Rev. Kurtz.

Questions for Discussion

1. Do you think Jack wants to talk about his brother or about himself? Or both?

2. Do you think Rev. Kurtz, as a youth minister, listens to Jack in an effective way? Would you have been satisfied with the conversation if you had been Jack? Why or why not?

3. Why do you think Jack has not gone to his brother with some of his questions?

4. Do you think parents should ever disown their children?

5. How do you think the brother feels about losing his family?

6. Do you think homosexuality is inherited? Why or why not?

PREGNANCY

I May Be Pregnant

The action occurs at a fast food restaurant after school. **Julie** *has asked her friends* **Fern** *and* **Odella** *to stop in so she can talk to them.*

Fern: So what's this all about?

Julie: You know I've been dating for about a year now.

Fern: Lucky you. Mom says I have to wait till I'm in high school.

Julie: Maybe that's not such a bad idea.

Odella: Why, for goodness sake? I thought you liked all the freedom.

Julie: I guess so.

Fern: You really sound down.

Julie: Yeah, well, I am.

Odella: Is there something you want to talk about?

Julie: I thought I did when I asked you two to meet me here. But now I'm not so sure.

Fern: We're your two best friends, Julie. If we can't trust each other, nobody can.

Julie: Things have become really messed up.

Odella: In what way?

Julie: I missed my period, you know? And I'm scared.

Fern: Has this ever happened before?

Julie: Not since the beginning.

Odella: Maybe it's just something that happened—missing the period, I mean. It sometimes happens to me. If you're under a lot of pressure or feel stressed out. Or maybe even if you're sick. All kinds of things can affect it.

Julie: You don't understand. Brad and I have... Well, we've been having sex. All the time now.

Fern: I'm not trying to be nosy, but did you use—

Julie: Condoms?

Fern: Yes.

Julie: Brad wanted to, but I couldn't. My church doesn't believe in birth control.

Odella: What are you going to do?

Julie: I don't know. I haven't told anyone yet, except you two. I'm not ready for a baby. I know a lot of kids think it's great, that it makes them important or something. But I don't want a baby.

Odella: Have you... Well, have you thought of an abortion?

Julie: Come on, Odella. I told you. My church doesn't believe in birth control.

Odella: OK, so maybe there are other options.

Fern: Like adoption.

Julie: I don't know what to do.

Fern: Maybe you aren't pregnant.

Julie: And maybe I am.

Odella: What about Brad? Will he stand by you?

Julie: Oh, wow, I don't know. You see, it isn't just Brad.

Odella: What do you mean?

Julie: What do you think I mean? It's other guys too. Other guys I've been with.

Odella *is hurt by Julie's reaction.*

Julie: I'm sorry. I'm just worried. I have no idea what to do.

Fern: Oh, Julie, I'm sorry. I'd help if I could, you know that.

Odella: Me too. If there's anything I can do...

Julie: I know. But it's my problem. I have to work it out myself. Anyhow, thanks for listening.

Questions for Discussion

1. How do you think Fern and Odella could have been more helpful to Julie?

2. Do you think Julie thought she could not get pregnant? Discuss why some girls think it could happen to someone else but not to them.

3. If Julie is pregnant, do you think Brad should be told that he may be the father of the baby? Why or why not?

4. Do you think Julie should immediately tell her parents? What do you think their response would be?

5. How do you think a pregnancy will affect Julie's schoolwork?

My Parents Will Never Understand

The action takes place at Keely's house.
*She and **Beth** and **Joy** are outside,*
sitting around the pool and talking.

Beth: You two are lucky, you know? You have parents you can talk to. Moms and dads who'll listen.

Keely: I agree. I am pretty lucky.

Joy: I feel the same way. I know a lot of kids complain about their parents. But I'm glad I have the ones I do.

Beth: Not me. It's like my parents have my life all planned out. I'm supposed to do this; I'm supposed to act like that. Why didn't they just build a robot? Then they'd be happy; it would do just what they want.

Joy: It sounds like you're having a problem.

Beth: You can say that again.

Keely: Do you want to talk about it? I'll be glad to listen. And Joy too, I'll bet.

Joy *nods.*

Beth: Nobody's going to understand. My parents want me to go to college and be an attorney or something. Then finally I'll get married, but only to the right man. Someone they'll want to pass judgment on, I'm sure. Or even pick out themselves. (*She begins to cry*) Well, it just isn't going to work out that way.

Joy: What do you mean?

Beth: I'm pregnant, that's what I mean.

Keely: Are you sure?

Beth: Yes, I'm sure. I went to a doctor; I'm nearly three months along. I know exactly when it happened.

Joy: I'm sorry, Beth.

Beth: The problem is, how do I tell my parents? They'll never understand. They have this little corner all picked out for me to fit in, and I'm supposed to do exactly what they say. Do you know that they've already enrolled me in daddy's college, for heaven's sake? They have my whole life laid out.

Keely: That's really rough.

Beth: I'll bet you guys' parents would understand if either of you got pregnant. But mine never will.

Joy: Well, my parents listen to me, and we compromise on a lot of things. But if I were pregnant, I don't know what they'd say.

Keely: Ditto for me.

Beth: Even before I think of what I'm going to do, I have to tell them. I'm afraid they'll kick me out, afraid they'll disown me or something. If they even bother to listen.

Keely: You really have a problem, don't you?

Beth: And no matter what, it isn't going to solve itself very easily. No matter what I do.

Questions for Discussion

1. Do you think Beth got pregnant because she was rebelling against her parents' making all of the plans for her life? Why or why not?

2. If you were in Beth's place, how would you tell your parents? Do you think they would be supportive?

3. Beth says she is afraid that her parents will kick her out or disown her. If they did, where could she go for help?

4. Do you think Beth's pregnancy will have any effect on Joy and Keely in their future dating relationships?

RACE

Moving to a New Country

*The action takes place in a social studies class
studying other cultures.*

Mr. Muller: So we see that there are a lot of different cultures and a lot of different ways of looking at things. Does anyone want to make a comment?

Kelly: We have several different cultures represented right here in class, don't we?

Mr. Muller: As a matter of fact, we do. We can't even say that there's one overall culture or way of looking at life in the United States. We have different nationalities represented and different religious and ethnic groups. And many who've come here have a difficult time adjusting to our general way of life. Yes, Farid, you wanted to comment?

Farid: I know I had a rough time, even though I was just a little kid. My parents still hang on to many of the old ways. They observe many of the customs and hold many of the beliefs our family had in Saudi Arabia.

Siang Yang: I understand. It was very difficult for me. When I came here, I didn't even speak the language. I've learned a lot in two years.

Edward: I'll bet it was rough at first. It was for me just moving from one part of the country to another.

Siang Yang: In my own country, I was an excellent student. Here I could barely get by. Everything was different, even the alphabet.

Kelly: Didn't you have anyone to help you?

Siang Yang: I didn't know anyone at first. Later, of course, I found other students who spoke my language and helped me understand how things were supposed to be done here.

Kelly: How did you manage at all?

Siang Yang: (*Smiles*) Not very well. I remember I found the restroom and tried to hide there, but decided I was just being a coward. The sooner I learned all I could about my adopted country, the better it would be for me.

Farid: Didn't you have any brothers or sisters?

Siang Yang: One older sister, already married. She came here too. And a brother in high school. We tried to help each other. (*Laughs*) He'd tell me something totally unbelievable he discovered every day, and I'd tell him something else.

Edward: It looks like you're doing OK.

Siang Yang: Now I am. But I was about ready to give up. I told my father I hated school and didn't want to go.

But he told me he'd come to this country to give the family the opportunity we didn't have back home, and I'd better make the best of it.

Kelly: I can't even imagine how hard that would be.

Siang Yang: The first day, I wanted to turn into smoke and disappear. But I didn't. And now things are better.

Mr. Muller: Thanks for sharing that with us. I'm sure we can all appreciate better now what every foreign student goes through in a new country. Especially, when so much seems different.

Siang Yang: Yes, I hope so. I wouldn't want anyone else to go through what I did.

Questions for Discussion

1. Are other cultures represented in your group? If so, ask each person to share how their culture is different and similar to others' in the group.

2. Farid says that his parents still observe many of the customs of their original country. Talk about how students raised in this country can better communicate with their parents who were raised in another culture, especially when the expectations of the parents' customs may conflict with the customs of their new homeland.

3. Siang Yang relates that he felt so strange in his new country that he found the restroom and tried to hide there. How can students reach out to new students more so they will not feel so alone?

4. Have you visited a country where another language was spoken? How did you feel when you could not communicate with someone because you did not speak the language?

Prejudice Kept Him Off the Team

*The action occurs on the school baseball field
where* **José** *is sitting by himself on the players'
bench. In a moment* **Kevin** *and* **Shelly** *enter,
see him and cross over to him. Just afterward,*
Umberto *enters and crosses to the others.*

Shelly: What's the matter, José? You look like you've lost
your last friend in the world.

José: Not that bad. But close enough.

Kevin: What is it? What's wrong?

Umberto *enters.*

Umberto: *Buenos tardes.*

José: Hi, Umberto.

Umberto: Something troubling you?

Shelly: Shouldn't you be with the rest of the team?

José: I'm going to quit the team, I think.

Umberto: A good player like you. Why would you want to do that?

Kevin: I don't understand. You're the best shortstop in the league.

José: So they tell me. (*Shrugs*) So why wasn't I chosen for the All-Star Team? Can anyone tell me that?

Umberto: Sure, José, I can tell you. Just look at yourself in the mirror.

Shelly: What do you mean, Umberto?

Umberto: It's pretty obvious. I went to the game too. Did you see any other Hispanics on the team?

Kevin: You're right, I didn't. I didn't give it much thought.

José: Yeah, well, I should have been there. And so should a couple of other guys I can think of as well.

Shelly: Do you think it was deliberate?

Umberto: What else?

Kevin: Couldn't it have been a mistake of some kind?

José: What sort of mistake?

Kevin: I hate to think that kind of thing goes on.

Shelly: Not just on the team either, I'm sure of that.

José: I've seen it a few other places too. Like when all of us, my mom and dad and my brother, go to a restaurant. I see the looks people give us.

Umberto: That's right, man. It's everywhere. This...thing about race. (*He looks at* **Kevin**) You should know about that stuff, right?

Kevin: You mean because I'm black?

Umberto: What else?

Kevin: (*Shrugs*) Yeah, things are supposed to be so much better now, but I'm not sure they are.

Shelly: At least there are some other black kids on the team. But you know what? There weren't any Asians, were there?

Umberto: (*Turning to* **José**) So what are you going to do?

José: You mean about the team?

Umberto: That's right. I wouldn't let this pass.

Shelly: How can you get anyone to listen?

Umberto: I don't know.

José: We'll just get into trouble if we raise a stink about it.

Shelly: It's a bad thing—if it's true.

José: It's true all right. Believe me, it's true.

Questions for Discussion

1. Have any of you ever felt like you were a victim of prejudice? Can you tell about it?

2. What should students do when they feel like they have been treated unfairly?

3. Do you think that José may not have made the All-Star Team for other reasons? Have you known anyone who blamed all of his or her failures on other people's prejudices when, in fact, that wasn't the reason at all?

4. If José quits the team, he might be jeopardizing a college scholarship. What are some others things he might be giving up if he quits?

SCHOOL

No Money for After-School Sports

The action takes place on the soccer field just after the first practice of the season. **Jeff** *has been watching from the sidelines.* **Cedric** *and* **Brandon** *head over toward him.*

Cedric: Jeff, why aren't you playing this year?

Jeff: I don't know.

Cedric: You're one of our best players.

Brandon: Yeah, Jeff, what's going on?

Jeff *shrugs.*

Brandon: Did something happen with the coach?

Jeff: Nothing like that.

Cedric: Coach misses you, Jeff. He even said so.

Jeff: I can't help it. I have a good reason for not playing.

Cedric: Oh, yeah?

Jeff: Right.

Cedric: OK, well, I'll see you guys. (*He exits.*)

Brandon: So come on, Jeff. What's up? I know how much soccer means to you.

Jeff: Maybe I just lost interest.

Brandon: And maybe you didn't. Does it have something to do with your mom and dad getting a divorce?

Jeff: You might say so.

Brandon: You're not moving or anything, are you? You're not going to go live with your dad?

Jeff: Nothing like that.

Brandon: Are you going to tell me?

Jeff: I guess I owe you.

Brandon: So come on.

Jeff: I don't have the money.

Brandon: What money?

Jeff: For the registration fee. It's a lot more than I have, a lot more than I can get. You know things were pretty bad before the divorce. With money, I mean. That's part of the reason Mom and Dad split up.

Brandon: It's not very much. Twenty-five dollars.

Jeff: I know, Brandon. But my mom says she doesn't have anything extra. Just enough for food and rent and stuff like that.

Brandon: There's nothing you can do?

Jeff: I thought of getting a job. Being a paperboy or something. But I couldn't get the money soon enough. By the time I earned that much, the season would be half over.

Brandon: Oh, man, I hate this. You're my best friend. (*Smiles*) If you were on the team, we'd be... invincible. Nobody, and I mean nobody, could get to us then. We'd go undefeated.

Jeff: You wish.

Brandon: Yeah, I do.

Jeff: Me too. But there's nothing I see that I can do about it.

Brandon: I know. I'd lend it to you if I could. Or I could ask my mom.

Jeff: I wouldn't want you to do that, Brandon. I'd never be able to pay you back.

Brandon: I just thought I'd ask.

Questions for Discussion

1. If Jeff knew that money was available for situations like his, he would probably request it. Do you know of funds in your community that are available to help people like Jeff?

2. Brandon is insistent that Jeff tell him what is wrong. Do you think he should have been? Could he have been more helpful?

3. Discuss some of the feelings that Jeff must have had when his mother told him there wasn't enough money for him to play.

Getting Ready for Graduation

The action takes place in an English class,
near the end of the school year.

Mr. Clark: We have some extra time today. Is there anything you'd like to talk about?

Lyle: I don't know about anyone else. But the thought of graduating and going on to high school scares me.

Perry: I agree. Here everything is familiar. We know the teachers and we know the routine. We're familiar with the schedule and the campus. Next year we'll be swallowed up.

Elizabeth: What bothers me is that we're going to be split up. Going to different high schools. Some of you I've known since first grade, and we very well may never see each other again. Unless we just happen to meet at the mall or something.

Melissa: Yeah, and then it won't be the same. I know. It's like when I left my old school and vowed to keep in touch with all my friends there. But I didn't.

Mr. Clark: But you made new friends, found new interests.

Melissa: You're right, Mr. Clark. But I really liked my old friends too. And now it's like I hardly ever think of them anymore.

Joanne: I'm afraid of just being swallowed up. All of the high schools are so big compared to lowly Washington Junior High. Here I felt like a person; I'm afraid there I'll just be a nothing.

Lyle: You could never be a nothing, Joanne.

Perry: (*In a chant*) Lyle likes Joanne; Lyle likes Joanne.

The rest of the class laughs.

Mr. Clark: All right now. Are you sure you're ready for high school?

Elizabeth: Seriously, Mr. Clark, I don't know if I am. Like Joanne said, here we're somebody. We're the top of the heap. The other kids look up to us. There—wherever "there" is—we'll have to start all over again.

Mr. Clark: But would you want it any other way?

There is a chorus of "Yeahs."

Elizabeth: Maybe not, but it's going to be hard.

Mr. Clark: Yes, it is. I won't downplay that part of it. But you'll get along; you'll get used to it. Millions of others have. And then before you know it, you'll be at the top of the heap once more.

Lyle: And then we'll graduate, and everything will change again.

Mr. Clark: That's how the world advances, Lyle. If it weren't for things like that, we'd still be back in the Stone Age.

Perry: Maybe that wouldn't be so bad, chasing saber-toothed tigers and woolly mammoths.

Mr. Clark: One thing we can't do is turn back the clock. No matter how much we'd like to do it.

Perry: Well, I'm kind of looking forward to it, you know. I want to be a scientist. So I want to take chemistry and physics and that kind of thing. I have to go to high school to do it.

Mr. Clark: And later to college. And that's how it's supposed to be.

Melissa: Well, I'm still scared. I still don't want to give up all my friends.

Mr. Clark: I know you don't, and I can sympathize. What about me? Every year a new group of kids comes along, and a few years later I lose them.

Perry: You really care about that? I didn't think teachers cared so much.

Mr. Clark: Don't you think I get scared too? On that first day of class, facing a group of young people I've never seen before. Change scares everybody.

Perry: But that's the way it works, right?

Mr. Clark: That's the way it works.

Melissa: So I guess we just have to accept it.

Perry: I guess we do.

Questions for Discussion

1. Can you relate to what the students are feeling and saying? Do you have some of the same concerns? What are other concerns that you have that are not mentioned?

2. Mr. Clark keeps trying to reassure the students that everything will be all right for them when they go on to high school. Do you think he is more concerned with reassuring them than listening to their needs and fears? How could he have been a better listener?

3. Elizabeth says that what bothers her is that the class would be splitting up. Do you think students who go to different high schools keep their junior high friends? Do you plan to?

4. What things can you do before you graduate that will make the transition to high school easier for you?

How to Find a Peer Group to Fit Into

The action takes place outside school after class.
*Ellie is talking to her brother **Burke** as they*
walk home from school. They had moved to the
new school less than a month earlier.

Burke: So how's it going, Sis?

Ellie: I wouldn't tell Mom and Dad, but I don't like this
school very well.

Burke: You don't? Why not?

Ellie: Everything's different...and bigger.

Burke: Is that so bad? I'm used to it by now, I guess.

Ellie: I'm not. I haven't really made any friends. How
about you?

Burke: I'm doing OK. So what do you think the problem
is?

Ellie: Trying to fit in. I mean I could fit in, but I don't have much in common.

Burke: How do you mean?

Ellie: Well, I tried two different groups, and I felt uncomfortable with both of them.

Burke: Why? What was so bad about them?

Ellie: The popular kids, for one thing. They have better clothes and more money and all that. I mean they were willing to be friends. At least I think they were. But I don't move in those kinds of circles. Mom and Dad aren't that rich.

Burke: I see what you mean. Maybe I was lucky to find a group of guys right off that I liked. I had no problems. But, yeah, I can see that there are other groups I wouldn't fit into. See, things got off to a good start for me. The guy next to me in homeroom offered to show me around. I took him up on it, and I met his friends.

Ellie: That's good.

Burke: But it doesn't solve your problem, right?

Ellie: Maybe I'm making too big a thing of this. Maybe I shouldn't try so hard.

Burke: You said there was another group.

Ellie: They're a little too much for me. Most of them smoke and some use drugs.

Burke: So what are you going to do?

Ellie: What I'd like to do is go back home.

Burke: Well, Sis, let's face it, this is home.

Ellie: If I can ever get used to it. You know what I wish?

Burke: What?

Ellie: That since we can't move back, I'd like to move all my friends here with us.

Burke: That would solve the problem, wouldn't it?

Ellie: But that's just wishful thinking. The only thing I can do, I guess, is keep on trying to find a group that I can be comfortable with.

Burke: I suppose that's right.

Questions for Discussion

1. Is Ellie doing the right thing in continuing to look until she finds a group that she can feel comfortable in? Have you had a similar experience?

2. Do you think Burke found his group faster because a friend from homeroom offered to show him around? Would you do the same thing for a new student?

3. What do you think will happen to Ellie if she doesn't find a group that she feels comfortable in? Do you think she will join a group unlike herself? Which group?

4. Ellie would like to go back to her old school where her old friends are. Have you ever felt like that? How did you overcome it?

Didn't Make the Squad

The action takes place at Jo's home.
She and **Lucy** *are in Jo's room.*

Lucy: I wish there was something I could do to make you feel better.

Jo: (*Crying*) There's nothing anyone can do.

Lucy: Will talking about it help?

Jo: There's nothing to talk about. I didn't make the cheerleading squad, and I just want to die.

Lucy: It can't be that bad, Jo.

Jo: (*Wiping her tears*) Oh, sure you can say that. *You* made the squad!

Lucy: Right now I wish I hadn't. It won't be any fun without my best friend being there too.

Jo: For days, weeks, we practiced those routines together. We both could do them in our sleep. (*Starting to cry* *again*) I just don't understand what happened. I didn't mess up, not once! Tell me, Lucy, what happened?

Lucy: I don't know. I honestly don't. I watched you and you looked great. I didn't think Helen had a chance. She's new, and she's not very well known around the campus.

Jo: But she could kick real high. In fact, I was shocked at how high. She must have been taking dance lessons all her life. Oh, why did she have to move here!

Lucy: Maybe she'll fall and break one of those long legs.

Jo: (*Snickering*) Wouldn't that be funny? (*Pauses—looks sad again*) But that's not likely to happen.

Lucy: Well, let's look at it like this. After next year, we'll be in high school. I think being on the squad in high school will be a lot more fun than this coming year will be. We can practice different routines all year. Then we will both try out for the high school squad this time next year. I know you'll make it then.

Jo: (*Brightening up*) Do you really think so?

Lucy: Of course I do. Next year will pass real fast. Then we will be on the high school squad together.

Jo: I hope so. I don't think I could take not making it again.

Questions for Discussion

1. Lucy went to Jo's house to comfort her. How do you think Lucy felt when Jo didn't make the team?

2. Jo can't believe she wasn't chosen. Have you ever had a similar experience?

3. Do you think Helen was chosen because she could kick higher than Jo, or is there another reason?

4. Do you think squad leaders may not want close friends on the same squad? Why or why not?

5. Do you think Lucy and Jo will remain friends the next year even though Lucy will be involved in activities that do not include Jo?

I Don't Want To Go

The action takes place at lunchtime on a school campus. **Wendall** *is sitting alone at a table.*

Bob: (*Entering and sitting down next to* **Wendall**) Hi, there. I noticed you made it to math class today.

Wendall: You noticed?

Bob: Sure did. Couldn't put my feet on your chair like I usually do.

Wendall: Tomorrow you can go back to it.

Bob: You mean you won't be back tomorrow?

Wendall: I doubt it. Not unless my old man is home sick again.

Bob: When your dad is away at work you stay home.

Wendall: A lot of the time—when he drives his rig across country he's gone for days.

Bob: What does your mom say?

Wendall: No mom around.

Bob: You're really alone when your dad's away.

Wendall: I don't mind. I have a lot of videos. Some of them I watch over and over.

Bob: But doesn't the school call your house? I know they called one day when I was home sick.

Wendall: They used to, but I think they've about given up. My dad was never there to return their calls or go to the conferences they set up.

Bob: And they let him get away with it?

Wendall: One time they turned him in to the authorities, but the judge said that I looked in good shape. He asked me where I wanted to live, and I told him with my dad. So he sent me back home.

Bob: But don't you get bored at home all day?

Wendall: Not nearly as bored as I get at school. I never know what's going on when I do go to class.

Bob: That's because you're always absent when the teacher's explaining things.

Wendall: Maybe so. Anyway, I just don't want to go.

Bob: But what about your future? My mom says everyone needs a diploma to get a job.

Wendall: I'll find something to do when the time comes.

Bob: Do you think you'd like school better if I helped you to catch up in some of your classes? So you'd know what was going on.

Wendall: Why would you want to do that?

Bob: I don't know. Just thought I'd ask.

Wendall: You mean you care one way or another if I go to school?

Bob: Sure I care. My dad says everyone should have a good education and nothing should stand in the way. If being behind is standing in your way of going to classes, then I'd be glad to help you get caught up.

Wendall: Are you one of those peer helpers? One of those people who cares about their peers?

Bob: Yes, I am.

Wendall: That's why you came and sat down by me?

Bob: I came and sat down because I wanted to. We aren't required to help. We do it because we want to.

Wendall: That's a switch. I'm not used to a person doing something for me because they want to. I'm not really someone all that great to be around.

Bob: I like talking to you. What do you say? Why don't we just give it try and see how it works out? I'll wait for you before school and we'll go to math class together.

Wendall: I'll think about it. If my old man is well enough to pull out in the morning, I may go to the beach.

Bob: I'll be waiting in front of the class.

Questions for Discussion

1. Why do you think Wendall doesn't want to go to school?

2. Does Bob do a good job in the way he offers to help? Why or why not?

3. What are some reasons kids are truant?

4. Do you ever try to help the person who is absent a lot?

5. Do you think Wendall will meet Bob the next day? Why or why not?

6. What does Wendall say that might make you think he has low self-esteem?

SEXUALLY TRANSMITTED DISEASES

How Could This Happen?

The action takes place in Dr. Marshall's office,
*where the doctor is talking with **Bryan**,*
president of the student council
at Roosevelt Junior High.

Dr. Marshall: Well, Bryan, I'm afraid I have some bad news.

Bryan: What is it, Dr. Marshall?

Dr. Marshall: Well, son, you have genital herpes.

Bryan: That's impossible.

Dr. Marshall: I'm afraid not.

Bryan: But I never...well, once, that's all. One time.

Dr. Marshall: I'm sorry.

Bryan: Can you do anything about it?

Dr. Marshall: It's easy to treat—the symptoms, that is—so you'll feel better. In fact, I'll give you a salve right away.

Bryan: That's all?

Dr. Marshall: Well, we'll try something else too. A systemic medication. One that gets to the core of the ailment.

Bryan: And if you try this medication, you can cure it?

Dr. Marshall: I'm sorry, Bryan, but I didn't say that.

Bryan: Well, you can, can't you?

Dr. Marshall: In a word, son, no. There's no cure.

Bryan: (*Frightened*) Does that mean I'm going to die? I'm not going to die, am I?

Dr. Marshall: (*Smiling kindly*) Just because something is incurable doesn't mean it's fatal.

Bryan: You mean I'm always going to have those blisters? And all the pain. Besides the blisters, the whole area hurts. Is it always going to hurt?

Dr. Marshall: Not at all. The blisters will appear irregularly. And you can see them and treat them. In boys or men, it's easier. In women, they're harder to detect.

Bryan: How am I going to tell my mom? She's going to hate me. And so is Dad. They're not going to believe it.

Dr. Marshall: Would you rather I tell them?

Bryan: No, sir, I'll do it. What if kids at school find out? How will that look? The president of the student council has a venereal disease.

Dr. Marshall: Why would they have to know? No one would tell them. I certainly wouldn't. Not only would it be unethical to talk about my patients, but I certainly agree that it's wrong.

Bryan: What about the...the girl?

Dr. Marshall: She definitely should see a physician. If I were you, I'd talk to her about it.

Bryan: Yes, I guess that's what I'll do. I want to ask you something else.

Dr. Marshall: Of course.

Bryan: Am I going to have this all my life? What if I want to get married? What if I want to have kids?

Dr. Marshall: Yes, you'll always have it. But much of the time it will be dormant. That means it won't be contagious if you're careful.

Bryan: Careful?

Dr. Marshall: Just don't have sex when you notice any blisters. Otherwise, it's OK.

Bryan: I'm just a kid, and I'm going to have this the rest of my life.

Dr. Marshall: Unless a cure is found.

Bryan: Do you think that's possible?

Dr. Marshall: Anything's possible. And I wouldn't be surprised if some day—maybe before too many more years have passed, that someone will come up with something that works.

Bryan: But until that time, I'm going to have blisters, and I have to be careful.

Dr. Marshall: That's about it.

Bryan: Thanks. At least it's not AIDS or anything like that. I just didn't think it would happen to me. To other kids, but not me. I still don't know how I'm going to tell Mom and Dad.

Dr. Marshall: I wish you luck, son. I don't envy you the position you're in.

Bryan: I know.

Questions for Discussion

1. Bryan did not think that he could get a venereal disease because he had engaged in sex only once. What other diseases can a person get the first time he or she has sex?

2. Congenital herpes does not have a cure. What could one do to keep from contacting it?

3. What approach would you use if you were in Bryan's place and had to tell your parents?

4. Do you think the girl will be surprised when Bryan tells her? Do you think she will look for the person who gave it to her?

5. Bryan asks the question, "What if the kids at school find out?" Do you think they will? Would you tell anyone if you were Bryan?

Will This Disease Keep Me from Getting Pregnant?

The action occurs at Nancy's home while both her parents are at work.

Nancy: I don't know what I'm going to do. I never believed something like this could happen to me.

Rochelle: You have an STD, you said.

Nancy: I went to the doctor yesterday, and I'm so upset I don't know what to do.

Rochelle: What is it?

Nancy: What!

Rochelle: I meant what disease do you have? Herpes or what?

Nancy: Gonorrhea!

Rochelle: Can't that be cured?

Nancy: It can be cured—if you know you have it. I didn't know for a long time. With a boy it's easy to tell. That's what the doctor said. But it's much harder to tell when a girl has it. It can cause all kinds of things to happen before you even know you have it.

Rochelle: You mean it's gotten that bad with you?

Nancy: It's bad.

Rochelle: What does that mean?

Nancy: Oh, Rochelle! (*She cries*) I may not be able to have any kids.

Rochelle: You may not? You mean maybe you can?

Nancy: The doctor wasn't sure. He said it had progressed pretty far, but we may have caught it in time. He said he's seen it this bad, and later the girls had babies, and it was OK. But at the same time, others had it about as bad as I did. When they tried to have kids, they couldn't.

Rochelle: Would that be so bad, not having kids, I mean?

Nancy: Rochelle!

Rochelle: Sorry. There's always adoption, isn't there? Or foster kids.

Nancy: But you know me. When I was a little girl, I used to dream of growing up and having a houseful of kids. And anyhow, who would want to marry me if I can't have kids?

Rochelle: Gosh, Nancy, that's a long way off. High school and maybe college.

Nancy: No! I made up my mind a long time ago that the most important thing I could do was get married and have kids. I don't want to go to college. Other kids dream of having a family, but it isn't so important. Don't you understand? If I can't have kids, nothing matters.

Rochelle: How can you find out? Can you go to another doctor? Can you have some sort of tests? Can you—

Nancy: I don't know! And maybe that's the worst part, not knowing. Even if it's always been my dream, maybe if I knew for certain one way or the other, it would be better.

Rochelle: I'm sorry, Nancy.

Nancy: I don't know why I let Terrence talk me into having sex. But I thought it would be OK. We were going steady and everything. I should have listened.

Rochelle: What do you mean?

Nancy: To what everyone said about having sex before you get married.

Rochelle: It isn't just AIDS, is it? Everyone talks about AIDS. But there are other STDs, as well. I wonder why nobody ever seems to talk about them much anymore.

Nancy: Maybe they should. Or I should have listened.

Rochelle: I wonder if Terrence knows.

Nancy: I'm not going to tell him.

Rochelle: But what if he has sex with other girls? What if he infects them too?

Nancy: Maybe. Someone should tell him. I wouldn't want any other girl to end up like this. I wouldn't want anyone else wondering whether they could ever have kids or not. It's not worth it.

Questions for Discussion

1. Rochelle uses the initials STD. What do they stand for?

2. Nancy is afraid that she will not be able to have children because of having an STD. What are some other sexually transmitted diseases which may alter one's life? In what way?

3. Nancy says, "I don't know why I let Terrence talk me into having sex." Why do you think anyone lets another person talk him or her into doing something they do not want to do?

4. Nancy says that someone should talk to Terrence. Why do you think she is not willing to do it herself?

SUICIDE

Too Much Stress

The action takes place in a hospital room.
Alexandria *has taken an overdose of sleeping pills. Her best friend,* **Whitney,** *is visiting her.*

Alexandria: Thanks for coming to see me, Whitney.

Whitney: Of course, I'd come to see you. Are you OK?

Alexandria: I'm OK. I just did a stupid thing, that's all.

Whitney: You must have had a reason.

Alexandria: I don't mean taking the pills was stupid. I really wanted to take them. I don't want to live anymore. I meant it was stupid that I didn't take enough pills to make me die.

Whitney: Alexandria, don't talk like that.

Alexandria: I probably won't do it again. I failed once. Just like I fail with everything else.

Whitney: What do you mean?

Alexandria: You know me, Whitney. I study all the time. I try to do what my parents want. But you know what my grades are. B's and C's. Not even a single A, except in gym, and who cares about that?

Whitney: I know you try hard. And that's a good thing, isn't it? I mean if I studied half as much as you do—

Alexandria: You'd have all A's, instead of mostly B's. Wouldn't you?

Whitney: Maybe, I don't know. But why are we talking about me?

Alexandria: I can't take the pressure. I can't live up to what my mom and dad want. I never cared about the things they have planned. I always thought I'd go to beauty school or something like that. Like my Aunt Audrey. Or work in a bank.

Whitney: I don't understand.

Alexandria: It seems like everyone's pushing me, trying to make me something I'm not. Ever since...

Whitney: Yes? What were you going to say?

Alexandria: Do you remember my brother?

Whitney: Don? Sure, I remember. It was a terrible thing.

Alexandria: That he died? That he fell out of that boat and got swept away.

Whitney: That was a long time ago. Three or four years. Why are you even thinking about that now? You should be thinking...I don't know, happy thoughts.

Alexandria: I'm not very happy, Whitney.

Whitney: Can I help?

Alexandria: I don't think anyone can help, except my family.

Whitney: What do you mean?

Alexandria: I told you. They have all these expectations. It's like when my brother died, they took everything they'd wanted for him and switched it to me. But I'm not Donald. I'm not like Donald at all. He was bright and popular. Good at everything. And what am I good at, can you tell me? Of course not. It's because I'm not good at much of anything.

Whitney: (*Taking Alexandria's hand*) You're good at being a friend. You're the best friend I ever had. I love you, Alexandria. I just about died when I heard what happened.

Alexandria: You're my friend too, Whitney. That's why I wanted to see you. Why I asked my parents to call. I can't talk to them. You know Mom. All she wanted to do was see if I was warm enough or had enough to drink or was going to listen to what the doctor said. Like I was a little girl and had a bad cold. And the whole time she was here, I felt I was being smothered, like I couldn't be me.

Whitney: I'm sorry.

Alexandria: I know. But I don't want to have the kind of life they want for me. It's like they're leading their own . lives through me. They have their own lives. Why do they want to lead mine?

Whitney: It's really that bad, huh?

Alexandria: Maybe even worse.

Whitney: Have you tried to talk to them about it?

Alexandria: Don't make me laugh.

Whitney: I wasn't trying to be funny.

Alexandria: I know you weren't. I was trying to be sarcastic, that's all. I'm just so tired.

Whitney: Do you want me to go?

Alexandria: Please don't, not yet.

Whitney: OK. I'll stay with you as long as you like.

Alexandria: Because if you go, I know Mom will be back. And Dad and Grandma and probably Grandpa too. And it'll start all over again.

Whitney: Could you talk to someone at school? A counselor...or your minister?

Alexandria: Maybe. Somehow it doesn't seem worth it.

Whitney: Don't talk that way, Alexandria. Please don't.

Alexandria: I'm sorry.

Whitney: Look, Alexandria, don't be sorry. I don't want you to be sorry. I want you to get out of here and be OK. I want things to be like they were.

Alexandria: I don't think they can be. Not ever again, you know?

Questions for Discussion

1. Why did Alexandria want to kill herself? Do you think the reasons she talks about were the real ones, or were there other problems?

2. Alexandria says that she could not take the pressure. What are some ways of dealing with stress?

3. Whitney seems to be a very good friend. Besides being there for her and being a good listener, what else could she do to help Alexandria?

4. Alexandria says that she doesn't think things can ever be as they used to be. What do you think she means by that statement?

It's My Fault

The action takes place at Ron's house.
Ron *is sitting in the living room with the drapes*
drawn so that the room is dark.
He is sitting on the sofa staring into space.
Dad *enters and sits beside him.*

Dad: Ron, aren't you going to go to school today?

Ron: I can't go, Dad. I can't face everyone.

Dad: Ron, it's not your fault. Sam made up his mind to...to kill himself, and you couldn't do anything about it.

Ron: That's not true. I knew he'd been depressed. He talked for weeks about wanting to end it all.

Dad: How could you have known he meant it?

Ron: He was my friend. The best friend I ever had, and I let him down.

Dad: I know how you must feel.

Ron: Do you?

Dad: No, son, maybe I don't. I never had anything like this happen. No one really close to me has ever died. And I know you two were close.

Ron: Since we were little kids. (*Trying to smile*) His mom used to call us her Siamese twins. I bet I felt as close to him as any twins ever felt to each other.

Dad: I'll bet you did too. And I know you're going to miss him.

Ron: I should have seen the signs. Talking about giving everything away. Wanting to give me his new bike. Splitting everything else up among his brothers and sisters.

Dad: Even his parents didn't see it.

Ron: Why did he do it, Dad? What makes someone do something like that?

Dad: A lot of reasons, I guess. Being depressed. Being ill. A lot of reasons.

Ron: I know he was lonely. He didn't have many friends except me. I feel like I let him down, Dad. But he let me down too. Sure, maybe I have more friends than he did. Maybe I'm in more activities. But I cared about him. I know his parents did too.

Dad: Sometimes we just can't understand why people do things like this.

Ron: I know he wanted to make the junior high basketball team and didn't. But that's not a reason to kill yourself.

Dad: Maybe he thought he'd failed in a lot of things. Could that be it?

Ron: That's what he said. But I don't know what else he failed at. He didn't get the best grades in school, but neither do I.

Dad: That's OK. My mom had a good attitude about that. She always said if it came down to a choice of straight A's or a happy kid, she'd take the happy kid.

Ron: I don't think his parents put a lot of pressure on him. Not that I know of Nothing like that.

Dad: People can put a lot more pressure on themselves, sometimes, than others can.

Ron: I guess. But I should have known. I should have known, Dad. And I could have done something about it. I could have told his parents. I should have tried to get him to talk to someone. But I thought he'd snap out of it. I feel down sometimes too, and then things always look better.

Dad: Everyone gets the blues now and then. And you had no reason to think it was anything other than that with Sam. OK?

Ron: I guess so.

Dad: Can I drop you off at school? We have just about time to make it.

Ron: OK.

Dad: Good. Just a minute and I'll get the keys.

Questions for Discussion

1. Ron feels guilty that he did not see the warning signs before Sam committed suicide. What are some of the signs that a person should be aware of? Which of these applied to Sam?

2. Should a person ever feel guilty because of the suicide of a peer? Why or why not?

3. Someone has said that suicide is a permanent solution to a temporary problem. Discuss what this statement means.

4. Ron says, "And I could have done something about it. I could have told his parents. I should have tried to get him to talk to someone." What else could Ron have done?

Bibliography

Boskind-White, M., and W. C. White, Jr. *Bulimarexia, The Binge/Purge Cycle*. New York: W. W. Norton and Company, 1988.

Bower, Sharon, and Gordon Bower. *Asserting Yourself*. Reading, Massachussetts: Addison-Wesley, 1976.

Brammer, Lawrence. *The Helping Relationship: Process and Skills*. Englewood Cliffs, New Jersey: Prentice- Hall, 1973.

Bruch, H. *The Golden Cage: The Enigma of Anorexia Nervosa*. Cambridge, Massachussetts: Harvard University Press, 1978.

Cassady, Marsh. *Acting Step-By-Step*. San Jose, California: Resource Publications, Inc., 1988.

_____. *Characters In Action: A Guide to Play-writing*. Lanham, Massachussetts: University Press of America, 1984.

_____. *Playwriting Step-by-Step*. San Jose, California: Resource Publications, Inc., 1985.

D'Andrea, Vincent, and Peter Salovey. *Peer Counseling Skills and Perspectives*. Palo Alto, California: Science and Behavior Books, 1983.

Egan, Gerald. *You and Me: The Skills of Communicating and Relating to Others*. Monterey, California: Brooks/Cole Publishing Co., 1977.

_____. *The Skilled Helper,* 3rd. ed. Monterey, California: Brooks/Cole Publishing Co. 1977.

Furstenberg, F., Jr; J. Menken; and R. Lincoln. *Teenage Sexuality, Pregnancy and Childbearing.* Philadelphia: University of Pennsylvania Press, 1981.

Garfinkel, P. E., and D. M. Garner. *Anorexia Nervosa: A Multidimensional Perspective.* New York: Brunner/Mazel, 1982.

Gray, H. D., and J. Tindall. *Peer Counseling: In- depth Look at Training Peer Helpers.* Muncie, Indiana: Accelerated Development, 1985.

Hebeisen, Ardyth. *Peer Program for Youth.* Minneapolis: Augsburg Publishing House, 1973.

Johnston, L. D.; J. G. Bachman; and P. O. O'Malley. *Highlights from Student Drug Use in America 1975-1981.* U.S. Department of Health and Human Services, Public Health Service, National Institute on Drug Abuse, 1982.

Kennedy, Eugene. *Crisis Counseling—The Essential Guide for Nonprofessional Counselors.* New York: Continuum Publishing Company, 1986.

Kubler-Ross, Elisabeth. *On Death and Dying.* New York: Macmillan Publishing Company, 1969.

_____. *AIDS: The Ultimate Challenge.* New York: Macmillan Publishing Company, 1987.

Levenkron, S. *Treating and Overcoming Anorexia Nervosa.* New York: Warner Books, 1982.

Loughary, W. John, and Theresa M. Ripley. *Helping Others Help Themselves.* New York: McGraw-Hill, 1979.

MacFarland, Kee, and Jill Waterman with Shawn Conerly, Linda Damon, Michael Durfee, and Suzanne Long. *Sexual Abuse of Young Children.* New York: Guilford Publications, Inc., 1986.

Myrick, Robert D., and Don L. Sorenson. *Peer Helping: A Practical Guide.* Minneapolis: Educational Media Corporation, 1988.

Peck, M. L. *Youth Suicide.* New York: Springer Publications, 1985.

Rogers, Carl. *On Becoming a Person*. Boston: Houghton-Mifflin Co., 1961.

Satir, Virginia. *Self-Esteem*. Milbrae, California: Celestial Arts, 1985.

Sturkie, Joan. *Listening With Love: True Stories from Peer Counseling*. San Jose, California: Resource Publications, Inc., 1987.

Sturkie, Joan, and Gordon R. Bear. *Chrisitian Peer Counseling: Love In Action*. Dallas: Word, Inc., 1989.

Sturkie, Joan, and Valerie Gibson. *The Peer Counselor's Pocket Book*. San Jose, California: Resource Publications, Inc. 1989.

_____. *The Peer Helper's Pocketbook*. San Jose, California: Resource Publications, Inc., 1992.

Sturkie, Joan, and Marsh Cassady. *Acting It Out*. San Jose, California: Resource Publications, Inc., 1990.

Sturkie, Joan, and Charles Hanson. *Leadership Skills for Peer Group Facilitators*. San Jose, California: Resource Publications, Inc., 1992.

Sturkie, Joan, and Siang Yang Tan. *Peer Counseling In Youth Groups*. Grand Rapids, Michigan: Youth Specialities/Zondervan, 1992.

Van Cleave, Stephen; Walter Byrd; and Kathy Revell. *Counseling for Substance Abuse and Addiction*. Waco, Texas: Word Books, 1987.

Van Ornum, William, and John B. Mordock. *Crisis Counseling with Children and Adolescents—A Guide for Nonprofessional Counselors*. New York: Continuum Publishing Company, 1983.

Varenhorst, Barbara. *Real Friends*. San Francisco: Harper and Row, 1983.

Wallerstein, J. S., and J. B. Kelly. *Surviving the Breakup: How Children and Parents Cope With Divorce*. New York: Basic Books, 1980.

A Quick Reference for Peer Helpers

The Peer Helper's Pocketbook

Joan Sturkie & Valerie Gibson

Paperbound, $7.95, 74 pages, 4¼" x 7", ISBN 0-89390-162-8

The Peer Helpers Pocketbook, by peer helping consultant Joan Sturkie and former peer helper Valerie Gibson, provides your students with a fast, handy
reference. This small book for pocket or purse gives
tips, a review of basic skills, and a section for important referral tele-
phone numbers—for those times when more help is indicated.

Teach Teens to Listen With Love

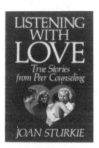

Listening with Love: True Stories from Peer Counseling, Revised Edition

Joan Sturkie

Clothbound, $17.95, 270 pages, 6" x 9", ISBN 0-89390-151-2
Paperbound, $11.95, 270 pages, 6" x 9", ISBN 0-89390-150-4

Teacher's Guide to Listening With Love

by Dr. Alisann Frank, edited by Joan Sturkie

Paperbound, $9.95, 64 pages, 5½" x 8½", ISBN 0-89390-161-X

Listening With Love is a book of issues universal
among young people today. It was created by Joan
Sturkie, a former high school counselor and peer
counseling teacher who now serves as a consultant
for school peer helping programs. In this book, Joan relates stories
from real students in actual classes that address specific problems and
the solutions that develop. Includes a chapter on how to start and
maintain a peer helping program in your school.

Listening With Love can be used as a text for a peer helping course.
The *Teacher's Guide to Listening with Love* will help you plan lessons
based on the text. For each chapter in the text, the guide presents an
opening lecturette, questions for post-reading, activity suggestions,
and a brief preview to get ready for the next lesson. The teacher's
guide gives you a way to focus the students on their own feelings about
the issues discussed in the stories in *Listening with Love.*

Order from your local bookseller, or use the order form on the last page.